A Shtikel Sholom

Also by Barak Hullman

Figure It Out When You Get There: A Memoir of Stories About Living Life First and Watching How Everything Falls In Line

A Shtikel SHOLOM

(*A Little Bit of Sholom*)

A STUDENT, HIS MENTOR AND THEIR UNCONVENTIONAL CONVERSATIONS

BARAK HULLMAN

A Shtikel Sholom
Copyright © 2018 by Barak Hullman

Published by Pike & Vagenheim

Stay updated about new books and speaking
engagements at www.barakhullman.com

Cover design by Barak Hullman
Book layout design by Barak Hullman
Typesetting by Oleksiy Serdyuk

ISBN: 978-0-9993896-2-1

I am not a teacher, but an awakener.

— Robert Frost

To my friend, mentor, rabbi and teacher
Sholom ben Yosef Yukesiel Zushe z"l and his wife Judy

To Sholom's children Mordechai, Abba, Miriam,
Bryna, Netzach, Nachi and Leah

May their lights shine bright

— Barak Hullman

Stories
Are a Window

Sholom Brodt is dead. It took me a lifetime to find him. It took me more time to understand and really appreciate him. Then he died. I'm still here, but Sholom has left this world.

After Sholom passed away at age 68 from pneumonia I started writing posts about him on Facebook. It started with one short moment in the 18 years we spent together as student and teacher. I didn't think anyone would actually read it, but my wife encouraged me to post the story. The response was surprisingly overwhelming.

Having just completed my first book, *Figure It Out When You Get There: A Memoir of Stories About Living Life First and Watching How Everything Falls In Line*, I was in the habit of writing stories. I continued writing and sharing short stories about Sholom and me for the next six months.

This book is a compilation of those stories. They are snapshots of the relationship between a student and his mentor searching together for answers about the meaning of life and for meaning in life.

When I first asked Sholom to be my rabbi and mentor (*mashpia*) he refused, instead making me a deal: "I'll be your friend and you'll be mine and we'll help each other out."

These stories are a window into how Sholom and I kept our deal.

Barak Hullman
Jerusalem 2018

All of the quotes and stories are from my memory. If anything is misquoted, it's my fault.

Photo credit: Aaron Hyman

Be Transparent
To Your Source

Sholom and I were learning on *Shabbos* morning. He paused with his finger still on the place where we were learning.

Sholom: "Barak, why are you so fat?"

Me: "Sholom, why do you look like you're 90 years old?"

He went back to the learning as if we'd never stopped.

When I first started my *chevruta* (learning partnership) with Sholom on *Shabbos* mornings I asked him all of my big questions.

Me: "Is there really an *Olam Haba* [the World to Come]?"

Sholom: "Yes."

Me: "How do you know?"

Sholom: "I know."

Me: "Everything you tell me I'm going to believe. If you say there's a World to Come then there is."

Sholom: "Let's start learning."

Me: "Wait! I have more questions."

Sholom: "Next time." Then tapping on the book we were learning from, "start reading."

Around eighteen years ago I contacted Reb Zalman Schachter and asked him in a long letter to be my rabbi. I wanted a teacher who was connected to Reb Shlomo Carlebach as close as possible. He told me directly, "There's no need to ever write me again. Sholom Brodt is in Nachlaot. You're in Nachlaot. Go to him." I didn't tell Sholom until many years later that Reb Zalman sent me to him, but when I did he was very pleased.

I knocked on the Brodt's door and Sholom asked me what I needed.

Me: "Hi Rabbi Brodt. I want you to be my rabbi and *mashpia* [spiritual advisor]."

He asked me to come inside.

Sholom: "I'm no one's rabbi and certainly not qualified to be a *mashpia*."

Me: "I don't care. I've decided you're my rabbi."

Sholom: "Let's start with my name. It's not 'Rabbi Brodt.' My name is Sholom. Don't ever call me rabbi again. Call me Sholom."

Me: "Okay, Sholom. How do we start the rabbi-student relationship?"

Sholom: "I'm not going to be your rabbi. I'll make you a deal. You be my friend and I'll be your friend and we'll help each other out. How does that sound?"

Me: "Sounds good to me. How do we start?"

Sholom: "I give a lesson on Wednesday nights. Come to that."

Me: "That's not enough. I want private time to learn with you."

Sholom: "Fine. I have 7:45 *Shabbos* morning available."

Me: "7:45! It's my only morning to sleep in."

Sholom: "Take it or leave it. That's the only time I have available."

I took it and that's how I merited to be able to write these stories.

S holom would ask, "What does it mean to be humble?"

His answer was "to be transparent to your source. When you give someone a glass of water they should know it's from *Hashem* [God] and not from you."

He often asked me to pour him a glass of water to teach me this lesson again and again. I poured water for him hundreds of times. He was always asking me, "Barak, can you please pour me some water," or just point to the glass. Every time in my head I'd repeat, *be transparent to your source, be transparent to your source.*

5

A close friend of mine from Jerusalem was getting married in New York at the same time I travelled there for business. Sholom was on a trip and would conduct the wedding. I got to the hotel the day of the wedding and saw Sholom standing outside smoking a cigarette.

I shouted "*shalom aleichem* [peace be upon you], holy brother" from the open car window and parked. I was so happy to see Sholom in the spiritual emptiness of America. I told him how strange it was to see him in New York. I'd never seen him outside of Israel before or since.

Me: "Isn't it so strange that we're here together in New York?"

Sholom shrugged his shoulders without saying a word, and took a drag on his cigarette.

Me: "Are you okay, Sholom?"

Sholom: "*Baruch Hashem* [thank God]. Take your bags inside. Do you need me to help you?"

I left Sholom smoking in the parking lot. Then I realized that although I felt like things were different meeting him in America, for him nothing had changed. Sholom was still in Jerusalem. He had taken *Eretz Yisrael* (the land of Israel) with him.

S everal years ago Sholom and I were sitting and resting after the dancing on *Simchat Torah* (the Jewish holiday celebrating the completion of one cycle of reading the Torah). We were tired and a little drunk. I turned to Sholom and said, "I love you so much, Sholom. You've done so much for me. I want to give you a gift."

He had a curious look on his face; eyebrows raised and eyes wide open.

Me: "When you die…"

Sholom interrupted me, "Maybe you'll die first?"

Me: "Thanks a lot. I'll take my chances. When you die everyone is going to say 'Oh what a great *tzadik* [totally righteous person]! Such a big rabbi! Oh rebbe, rebbe, rebbe!' "

He was serious now.

Sholom: "*Chas v'shalom* [God forbid]."

Me: "Exactly! When you die I'm going to shout at the top of my lungs, 'Sholom Brodt was not a *tzadik*!' That's going to be my final gift to you."

He was smiling and pointed at me, "I like that! You'd better do it! I'm counting on you. No one else would do that. I'm counting on you. You can't get out of this one."

Over the years he would say to me, smiling, "Do you remember your promise?" or, "I'm counting on you! You made me a promise."

I'd tell him, "Come on, you're going to have a long and healthy life. When you're 100 and I'm 78 I'll say it. We have a long time until then."

Sholom: "You made me a promise."

Then Sholom died.

One of the first things I said to my wife was, "What do I do now? I made him a promise."

"You can't say it," she said. "People won't understand."

"It's a once in a lifetime deal," I told her. "I either do it or regret it for the rest of my life. Do you think Sholom would want people calling him a *tzadik*?"

She knew the answer was no. Anyone who knew Sholom also knew he would never want to be called a *tzadik*, ever.

I was sitting in the van with Sholom's body at the funeral. I knew that no matter what I had to say something

It was getting late. The *chevra kadisha* (burial society) guys were impatient. I went to Simcha and told him I have to say something.

"We wanted you to speak but couldn't find you," he said. "There's no more time. The burial society wants to bury the body."

"It will take a minute. I have to say something. I promised Sholom."

He agreed to let me speak. And with that I fulfilled the promise I made to my sweetest friend, mentor and teacher who I loved with all of my heart and being.

C hana Mason called me to ask if I wanted to guard Sholom's body for *Shabbos* morning. I took the 6 am to 8 am slot so I'd have time to get to the *mikva* (ritual pool) and back to Mayanot to lead the *davening* (prayers) by 9:15 am. I left the house at 5:15 and got to the *Chevra kadisha* room at the Sha'arey Tzedek hospital by 6:05.

When the people there before me left I was there all by myself. I closed the door and started crying. I said *tehillim* (psalms), *davened* (prayed) and spoke with Sholom. I told him how much I missed him and how much I appreciated what he'd done for me. My life would not have been the same without him.

I started learning from his book *Exodus: The Model of Personal Liberation*. He wrote in the beginning that אנכי (God's name, "I") stands for "I have given my soul [over to you] in writing [i.e., in the Torah]." I realized that Sholom had also given us over his soul in writing through his book and close to one thousand hours of lessons online.

Then I looked at the clock. It was 7:45 am. My *chevruta* with Sholom on *Shabbos* mornings was always at 7:45 am. Without realizing it, I was sitting with Sholom learning Torah on *Shabbos* morning just like I would have done had he been healthy and not passed away.

I started singing and dancing; jumping up and down, throwing my hands in the air shouting, "Thank you *Hashem* for Sholom! Thank you for the gift of Sholom! Thank you! Thank you! Thank you!"

At that point I was able to stop crying...for a little bit.

M any times Sholom would come home exhausted from a trip abroad and that same night give a lesson. He had a soft voice and was very calm. People would fall asleep at his lessons. I trained myself over the years to stay alert, but it took years of practice.

Sometimes everyone in the class would fall asleep except for Sholom and me. He always said not to wake someone up during a Torah lesson since Reb Shlomo Carlebach taught that the reason a person would fall asleep during a Torah lesson is because his or her *neshama* (soul) needs to hear the lesson "without resistance."

The class then turned into a *chevruta*. But Sholom would be so wiped out from his trip that he'd fall asleep in the middle of a sentence. I was the only one left awake. I always let Sholom rest for a minute and then gently woke him up. He didn't even realize he had dozed off and continued from where he left off, while everyone else listened without resistance.

S everal years ago Sholom suggested that I start teaching a Torah class. I told him he was crazy. I had no right to teach Torah. He never mentioned it again.

It took me about three years until I was ready. I asked Sholom if I could teach the class at their house on Tuesday nights.

Sholom: "No. We don't have a slot on Tuesdays."

Me: "What about Sunday?" I knew the other nights had classes scheduled.

Sholom: "Judy and I are too exhausted to clean up the house after we worked so hard for *Shabbos*. We don't have classes here on Sunday. Go to Mayanot."

That took the wind out of my sails. I wasn't going to teach the class. I didn't want to anyway and this is the way that Sholom treats me when I'm finally ready? Forget about it!

A friend of mine, Michael Avraham, kept pushing me to teach the class. Six months later I arranged to give the class at Mayanot. The first class over thirty people showed up. I told Sholom and he was very pleased; both that I was teaching the class—at Mayanot—and that so many people came.

The next class six people came and the class after that four came. I was feeling down. I thought, what do I need this for? The first class so many people came and now just four? (Thank you to the people that came and still come!) But then I remembered how Sholom would teach classes with only one person there. Sometimes, on Wednesday nights, I was the only person who showed up.

If Sholom, who knew so much more Torah than I ever will, was willing to teach just one person then what am I complaining about? I continued giving the classes.

I shared all of my problems with Sholom: big and small.

I once told him that I felt like I was wasting my life since I spent so much time at work. I felt like I should have been learning Torah all day like some of my friends.

First Sholom told me that my obligation was just to learn five minutes in the morning and five minutes at night and that would be considered as if I had learned the entire day. Anything beyond that was precious in God's eyes. Also, many of those people who learn all day are not fulfilling their obligation. "If you're going to learn all day," he said, "you need to be really learning all day, and not taking long breaks. You also have to be focused on your learning all day. Most people can't do it. They should get a job."

Then he told me that there were some rebbes who insisted that their *Chassidim* open a business rather than have a salaried job so that they would learn what real faith in *Hashem* meant. "If you get your *parnasah* (livelihood) from a business, you know it's from *Hashem* and no one else. It's not like that with a salaried position.

"You see," he said, "what you're doing is greater than someone who is getting paid to learn all day. You really are developing your faith. And you're supporting your family; and having guests on *Shabbos*; and giving *tzedakah* (charity). That's what you should be doing. Don't be jealous of people who learn all day. They should be jealous of you!"

S holom always answered the phone during his lessons. He answered as if the call wasn't disturbing his lesson while those of us present waited for him to finish.

"Shalom," he'd say and let the person on the other side start to talk, then interrupt them by saying, "I'm just in the middle of giving a lesson. Can I call you back?"

The person on the other side of the line was usually surprised and apologized for the interruption. Sholom then returned to the lesson as if nothing had happened.

I used to joke with him that he was taking pizza deliveries. He'd answer the phone in the middle of a lesson and I'd shout, "Pizza delivery!" Sometimes he'd smile.

Even though I joked with him, I understood what Sholom was doing. He didn't want anyone to feel like he was ignoring them. It was better to answer the phone and tell them he'd call back than not take the call.

12

S holom would often come late to Mayanot on Friday nights. I'd see him when we were dancing around the *bima* (raised section where the Torah is read). He was constantly dragging people into the circle of dancers against their will (see *Likutey Moharan* II:23 כב). I don't know what made people agree, but no one ever escaped Sholom's request that they join the dancing.

I tried to do like he did at times, but wasn't as successful.

Me: "Sholom, how do you do it? What's your secret?"

Sholom: "They think I'm a *tzadik* because I have a big white beard," he said with a smile and a roll of his eyes.

I occasionally told Sholom that I did not feel like I a success. His answer was always the same. "You're a *neshama* and a part of God. Just focus on that.

"Not everyone has to be a *tzadik*. Who says having a lot of money is 'success'? You inspire a lot of people, including me. That's more important."

I've blown the *shofar* since I was a kid. People often give me compliments on my *shofar* blowing. One year I told Sholom that I asked the rabbi if he would let me blow the *shofar* for Rosh Hashana.

Sholom was upset. "You can't ask to blow the *shofar*! You have to be asked."

Me: "But I'm good at it."

Sholom: "So what? That's not the point."

Me: "I understand, but I'd really like to blow the *shofar* for Rosh Hashana."

Sholom: "You won't. The rabbi is blowing the *shofar* and that's not up for negotiation."

Me: "But I know I can do a better job than the rabbi."

Sholom: "And who says the community needs your *sho-far* blowing? They need the rabbi's *shofar* blowing! The (Lubavitcher) Rebbe hardly made a sound when he blew the *shofar*. Do you think you could do a better job than the Rebbe?"

I brought it up again the next year. He got angry at me as in the previous year. I brought it up again a third year and that's when he made it clear. I was in tears by the time he was finished rebuking me.

The next year Shlomo Katz lead the *davening* on Rosh Hashana at Mayanot. At some point he asked me if I had a "*taiva*" (craving) to lead the *davening* on Rosh Hashana.

"Once I did," I told Shlomo, "but Sholom took it all out of me. I don't have a desire to lead the *davening* or blow the *shofar* on Rosh Hashana any more."

"Pssss," Shlomo said. "How did he do that?"

I came to Sholom an unformed vessel and he molded me. Most times he was gentle; other times less so. Regardless, I kept coming back for more fixing.

E very time I was in a taxi with Sholom he would ask the driver, "What's the difference between your GPS device and *Hashem*?"

The driver would be confused. Sholom would continue.

"Both know where you are and where you want to go. Both give you directions. When you make a mistake, they both try to put you back on the right way. So, what's the difference between your GPS device and *Hashem*, the Master of the world?"

The drivers would usually say, "Nu?"

Sholom: "The difference is that *Hashem* cares. Your GPS doesn't care what you do, but *Hashem* does. He's always watching you and He always cares about you."

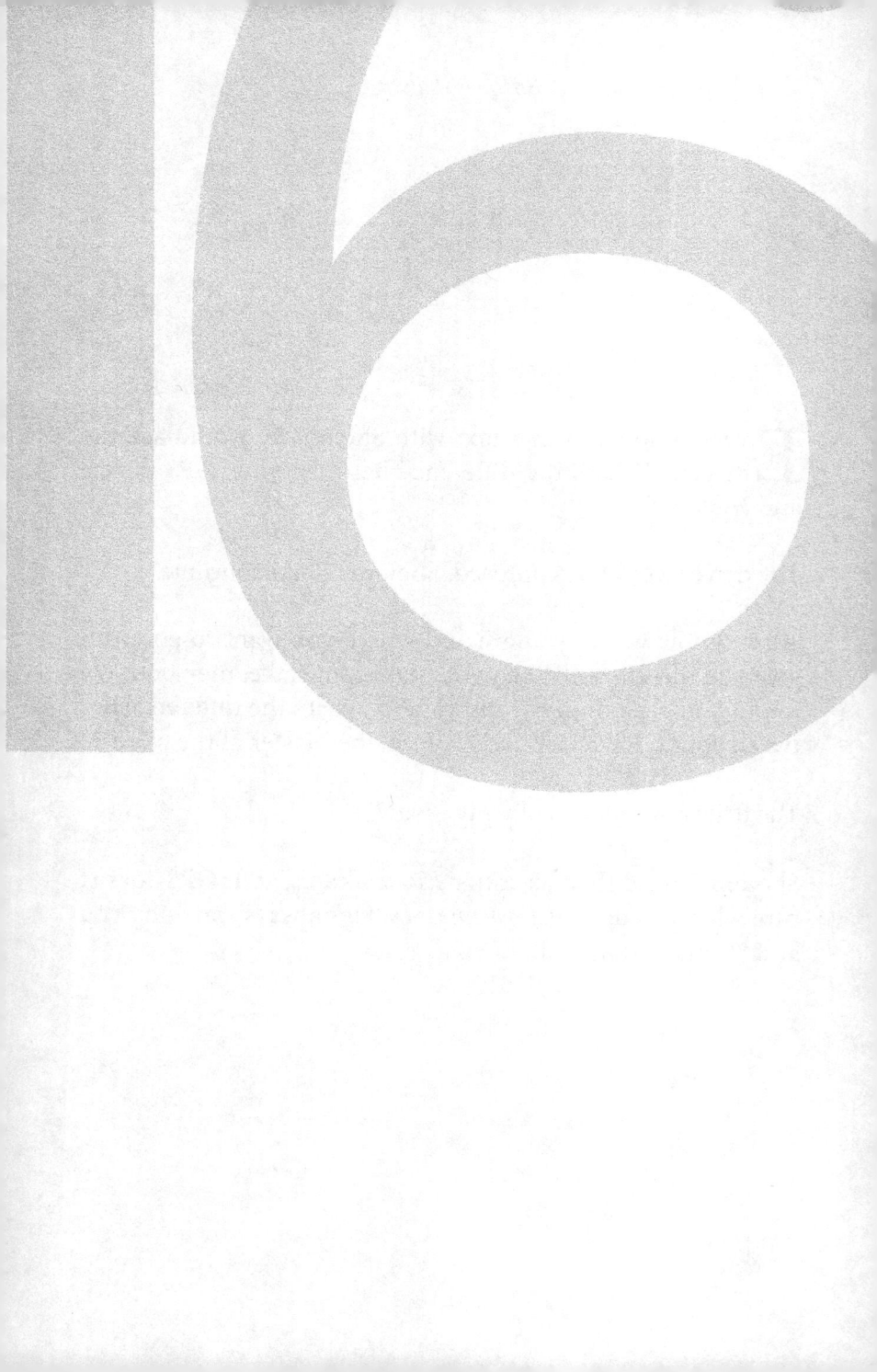

More than once it happened that there was someone in *shul* who was *davening* like crazy, out loud. I asked Sholom what I should say to people like that because it bothered my *davening* so much.

He told me I should ask *Hashem* to merit to *daven* like the crazy guy.

Me: "But I don't want to *daven* like him!"

Sholom: "So *daven* that you should want to. Wanting to want is also a certain level. And *daven* for me too. I want to *daven* like him, but haven't meritted yet."

S holom often used custom made examples during his lessons to make a point. He used this example many times when I was present.

Sholom: "Barak is an Eagle scout," he'd say with a big smile.

"What happens when a rope tears? You tie it back together, right? What knot would you use, Barak?"

Me: "Bowline."

Sholom: "You see! He really is an Eagle scout!

"What happens when you tie the rope together? Where is the strongest point?"

Me: "Where the knot is. The rope might tear in another place, but the knot won't come undone."

Sholom: "That's what happens when we do *teshuva* [come back to God]. We were separated from *Hashem*, but when we come back together the thing that separated us becomes the strongest point. What else happens?"

Me: "The two ends of the rope where the tear was are now closer together than before."

Sholom: "I see you've been paying attention in my lessons."

S holom taught that we don't say a *bracha* (blessing) before giving *tzedakah* because you might miss the opportunity and it's more important to just give the money.

Sholom: "But when you give the money look the person in the eye and smile. That's also *tzedakah*. Sure the person needs the money, but maybe he needs your smile even more?"

Are You A Jew Or A Rabbi?

19.

This is a story Sholom would tell every few years.

There was drunk named Vlad who once didn't have any money to get drunk. So he broke into the church. He knew there would be wine used for the *galach's* (priest's) services. Sure enough Vlad finds the wine. He gets drunk and sees a closet with the *galach's* robe and hat. He puts them on and eventually falls asleep.

He wakes up in the morning with a hangover, not remembering anything. He sees himself in the mirror dressed as a priest.

"Am I a priest?" Vlad says out loud. "I thought I was a drunk, but maybe I was always the priest!"

He has to figure it out. He knows that the *galach* can read, but Vlad the drunkard cannot. Vlad finds a book. He turns it up and down. He can't read it. So Vlad concludes, "Ah, what a secret he's been keeping. The priest also doesn't know how to read!"

Sholom would say, when you're looking at your own transgressions be honest. Don't fool yourself like Vlad the *galach*.

This is a story Sholom would tell before every Yom Kippur about when Reb Leibele Eiger (the grandson of Rabbi Akiva Eiger, from a family of *Misnagdim* [those that opposed the *Chassidim*]) became a *Chassid* of the Kotzker Rebbe. It was Yom Kippur, after the *davening* at night. Reb Leibele was learning and some of the Kotzker *Chassidim* were already laying on the benches in the *shul* sleeping.

One *Chassid* decided it was time to initiate Reb Leibele. He came over to his friend who was sleeping, holding a *kiddish* cup and a bottle of wine. He kicked the bench and woke up his friend.

"Hey, Yankele. Wake up! We have to make *kiddish*!"

Yankele wakes up, "What? Oh, sure, *kiddish*. Okay. Let's do it fast."

The other *Chassid* pours the wine and starts to say, "Savri rabbanan…."

Reb Leibele shouts, "Stop!"

"What?" says the *Chassid*.

"You can't make *kiddish* tonight! It's Yom Kippur!"

"So what?" asks the *Chassid* and continues, "*Savri rabbanan….*"

"Stop!" shouts Reb Leibele.

"What now?"

"You can't make *kiddish* tonight! It's Yom Kippur [a high holiday when Jews fast]."

"Prove it," says the *Chassid.*

"It's written in the *Shulchan Aruch* [book of Jewish law]."

He waves him off, "Ah, that's nothing," and he continues, "*Savri rabbanan....*"

"Stop!"

"What now?"

"You can't make *kiddish* tonight."

"Says who?"

"It says so in the Torah."

"The Torah? Eh, leave us alone." Holding the *kiddish* cup, "*Savri rabbanan....*"

"Wait! Stop!"

"What now?"

"You can't make *kiddish*!"

"Says who?"

"God. God says!"

The *Chassid* puts the cup down. "Oh, *God* says."

Sholom would say, "You see, by Kotzk it wasn't enough that it says so in the *Shulchan Aruch* or the Torah. You had to know that *Hashem* said it."

A few years, ago when I saw Sholom's health declining, I realized that one day I'd be without him physically in this world. So I made sure to ask him all of the questions I possibly could think of. Then I thought, when Sholom dies, so many people will wish they had spent more time with him. I had filled myself up with Sholom. It was like I had eaten all I could handle, and from that point on I was just enjoying the dessert.

I always wondered why Sholom's classes weren't filled to the brim with people standing outside. When I told him that, he mentioned Shlomo Katz and Avraham Sutton, and how they got big crowds but he wasn't sure why more people didn't come to his classes.

Me: "Where is everyone? They don't realize the amazing Torahs you're giving over. Just wait until you're in the next world, then they'll really appreciate you."

Sholom: "Maybe we need to promote it more on Facebook?"

Then he'd start the lesson with a *niggun* (*Chassidic* tune).

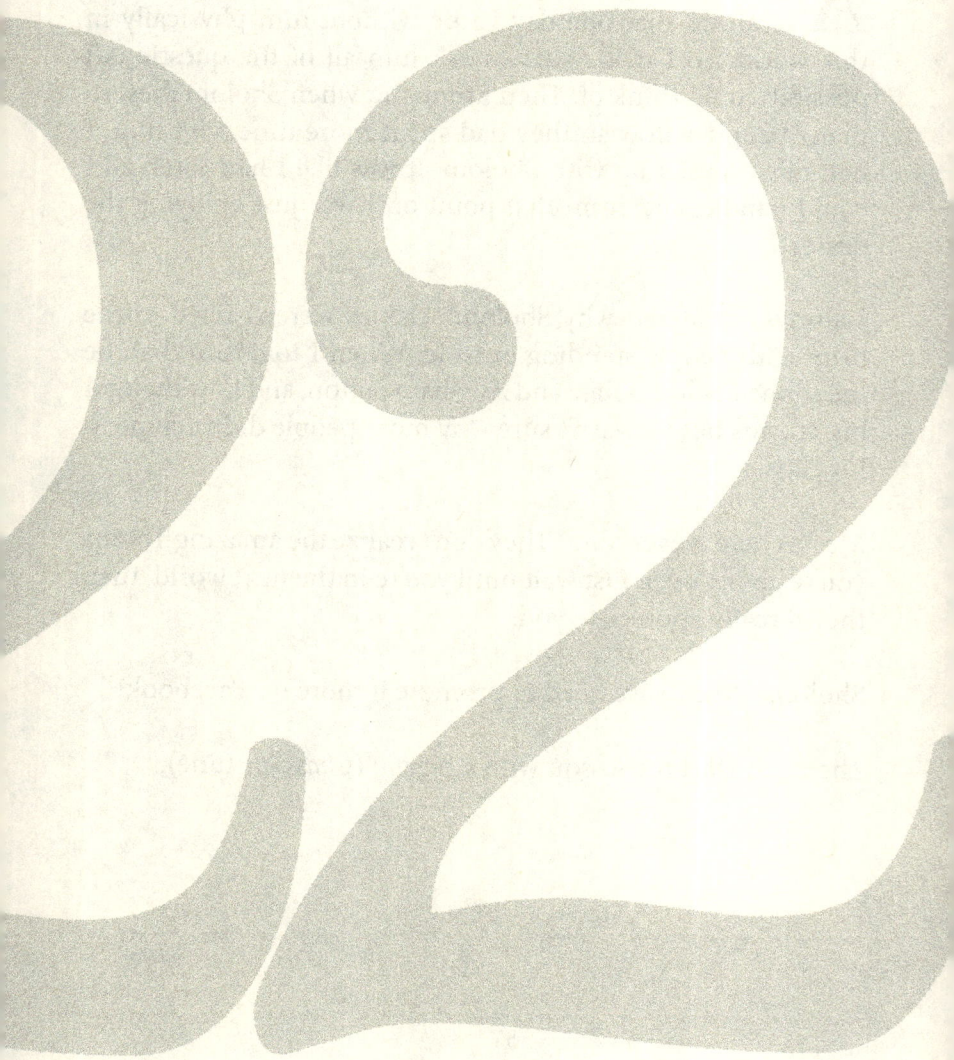

I once said to Sholom that I wasn't sure where I would want to live if the Lubavitcher Rebbe were still alive and going strong. Would I want to live in Crown Heights by the Rebbe or in Nachlaot with Sholom?

Sholom: "You wouldn't have that problem if the Rebbe was alive."

Me: "Why?"

Sholom: "The Rebbe would tell you where you needed to be."

S holom had very long *peyos* (religious sidelocks). They would reach almost to his waistline. He rolled them up and pinned them under his *kippah*. I onced asked him, "Why do you have such long *peyos*?"

Sholom: "Did you hear the story Reb Shlomo told about the guy in *Mea Shearim* [one of the most isolationist neighborhoods in Jerusalem]?"

Me: "No. I have no idea what you're talking about."

Sholom: "He once saw a *Chassid* in Mea Shearim with *peyos* down to his knees. Shlomo ran after the guy and asked him why he has such long *peyos*.

"The *Chassid* told him, 'My *peyos* are this long and my son's *peyos* will be shorter. His son's *peyos* will be shorter, until eventually my great grandchildren may not even have any *peyos*.' "

I told him that the Lubavitcher Rebbe didn't have long *peyos*.

Shrugging his shoulders Sholom answered, "You don't need long *peyos*. Shloime [our mutual friend Rabbi Gestetner] doesn't have long *peyos*."

That was the end of the conversation.

I once asked Sholom for advice on shaking women's hands.

Me: "Sometimes women stick out their hands and I'm not sure what to do."

Sholom: "You can bow and nod your head."

Me: "What if they insist?"

Sholom: "I'll shake their hand if they insist, but it's up to you. Do what you feel comfortable with."

Me: "What about hugging women?"

Sholom: "I don't hug women. Reb Shlomo did, but I don't."

Me: "What about when I'm leading the *davening* Friday night and I'm going around the *bima*, should I shake people's hands or will they think I just have a big ego?"

Sholom: "Shake their hands, but do it from a place of humility."

S ince I lead the *davening* at Mayanot, Sholom and I went over every single word of the *Shabbos davening*. He corrected all kinds of words I had pronounced incorrectly.

He would tell me, "You can't sing that *niggun* here, it has nothing to do with the words you're saying! Pick a *niggun* that fits the meaning of the words. Pay attention to the meaning of what you're saying."

After that he told me how I had to fit the breaks in the melodies to the breaks in the *davening*. That was particularly hard for me to get right. It took me years. There were times when he told me he couldn't stand the *davening* because I made the same mistakes so frequently.

We went over the melodies again together. I practiced them in my office during the week.

I'd look at Sholom after the *davening* on Friday night. He would shake his head. I had made a mistake...again. Finally one *Shabbos* I looked at him and he just smiled. No words. Just a smile.

I knew that if you wanted to be a student of Reb Sholom, you could not expect compliments. They would inflate an already big ego.

The only compliment he'd ever give me, and rarely, was telling someone in my presence that, "Barak leads the *davening* at Mayanot." I knew to stay silent and not say a word.

A Shtikel Sholom

Sholom considered himself a Chabadnik (a *Chassid* of the Lubavitcher Rebbe), but wouldn't wear a *kapote* (long black coat) or a black hat. There was a period during which I was considering wearing them.

Sholom: "I think you should wear a hat and *kapote*."

Me: "Why? You don't."

Sholom: "So what."

Me: "If you wear them, I will."

Sholom: "I'm not wearing a black hat!"

Me: "Then neither am I."

Sholom: "What about a *shtreimel* [fur hat]?"

Me: "I'll wear one if you do."

Sholom: "I actually own a *shtreimel* but I only wear it on Purim."

One *Simchat Torah* I noticed a new Chabadnik had joined the dancing. He was an older man who was clearly drunk. He was dancing with real gusto—in a black hat and *kapote*. All of sudden this new guy, who I hadn't seen at Mayanot before, grabbed me and pulled me into the circle of dancers. I knew he looked familiar. Then I realized that it was Sholom! He was wearing someone else's hat and *kapote*; having fluffed out his beard and then rolled it up. I couldn't stop laughing, but Sholom was dead serious.

I don't know why he wouldn't let himself wear a hat and kapote, but that *Simchat Torah* the hat and *kapote* that Sholom wore on the inside finally came out.

I n 2000 I was given a full scholarship to study in an online *smicha* (rabbinical) program. It was a year and a half long program. I printed up the material and studied it morning and night. I told Sholom and asked him to be my *smicha chevruta*. He agreed, telling me that it would be a good review for him.

It came time for the final test. Sholom tested me on the material. I was ready. The day after he asked me how it went.

Me: "I didn't take the test."

Sholom: "Why not?"

Me: "I realized that I don't really want to be a rabbi."

Sholom: "Neither do I."

Me: "Um, kind of late for that realization."

Sholom: "My father used to ask people: 'Are you a Jew or a Rabbi?' "

O nce I was coming home from *miluim* (IDF reserve duty) in my army uniform. I hated doing reserve duty. I was miserable. I passed by the Brodt's house as Sholom was standing outside smoking a hand rolled cigarette. He gave me an approving look and nod.

Sholom: "I didn't know you were in the army."

Me: "An artillery unit."

I just wanted to get home.

Sholom: "You know Reb Shlomo said soldiers [in the IDF] are not just *kodesh* [holy], they are *kodesh hakodeshim* [the holy of holies]."

S holom told me that when he would walk in the streets of Montreal with his black cap and poncho, the old Greek ladies would come over to him and kiss his hand while bowing down in front of him.

Me: "What? That's crazy. Why would they do that?"

Sholom: "They thought I was a Greek Orthodox priest. They didn't realize that I'm a Jew." Then he sighed. "That's my own fault."

One Wednesday night *parsha* (Torah portion) class Sholom introduced me to a nice older gentleman visiting from New York.

"This is Simcha Bunim. He's been a Reform rabbi for the past 40 years. He's learning in the yeshiva now."

I invited Simcha Bunim to our house for *Shabbos* lunch. We became good friends. He stayed in the yeshiva for a few months and then went back to New York, returning the next year.

I asked him why he chose to study at Simchat Shlomo of all the yeshivas in Jerusalem.

"Sholom was the only Orthodox rabbi that would accept me into his yeshiva. I tried them all, but no one would let me in. I lucked out, though. This is a wonderful place to learn and grow."

Under Sholom's guidance and friendship Simcha Bunim grew until he felt he could no longer be a Reform rabbi. We had a meal together before he returned to New York. He was trying to figure out what to tell his congregation.

The next year he came back he told me that he had left the Reform temple and was now studying at the Mayanot Yeshiva (Sholom helped him get in). Eventually he became a full fledged Chabadnik and started going on speaking tours.

I asked Sholom what he thought about Simcha Bunim becoming a poster child of Chabad—being interviewed in major newspapers and on TV—but that no one knew it was thanks to Sholom.

"Chabad doesn't accept me. I'm a Chabadnik, but because I don't wear a hat and a *kapote* I'm an outsider."

I told him the joke from Groucho Marx, "I sent the club a wire stating, 'Please accept my resignation. I don't want to belong to any club that will accept me as a member.'"

Sholom laughed, "Something like that."

31

When I first started learning with Sholom on *Shabbos* mornings he would have me read out loud from *Torah Studies* (*sichos* [talks] of the Lubavitcher Rebbe translated by Rabbi Sacks).

My reading voice was too loud. Sholom would tell me to lower my voice so I "don't wake up Judy." Gradually my voice would get louder again. Sholom would say, "Lower your voice. Why do you have to speak so loud?"

I got frustrated so I started imitating how Sholom spoke, very soft and calm. Then he was happy. If I spoke loudly again, I would return to the "Sholom voice" as soon as he hushed me. At first I did it just to please Sholom, but now I find myself using the "Sholom voice" on my own.

This is a story he would tell around *Shabbos* Bereshis (the first Shabbat of the year).

There were two brothers who eventually moved away from home and ended up in the same town. One brother was poor and lived on "the wrong side of the tracks." The other brother was wealthy and never visited his impoverished brother.

One day in *shul*, the rich brother heard that his father had been in town for a few days visiting his poor brother. The rich brother, shocked and upset, ran to the house of the brother on the other side of town. He entered the house and saw his father sitting there in his brother's run-down home.

"Father!" said the rich son, "why didn't you tell me you were in town?"

"Father?" said the father. "I'm your father?"

The rich son thinks, oy vey, my father is so old he doesn't remember that I'm his son.

"Yes, of course, father. You don't recognize me? I'm your son!"

"You're my son? Prove it."

"Prove it? What is this? Do you see that man over there?" pointing to the poor brother.

"Yes," said the father.

"Is he your son?"

"Yes," said the father.

"Well, I'm his brother. So, if he's your son and I'm his brother then I'm also your son."

"What?" said the father cupping his hand on his ear as if he could not hear.

The rich son said louder, "He's my brother! I'm your son!"

"What?" said the father cupping his ear. "I can't hear you."

Even louder this time, "That man is my brother and I am your son!"

Then Sholom would say in Yiddish what the father told his rich son: "אז א ברודער איז א ברודער-איז א טאטע א טאטע". *Az a bruder iz a bruder—iz a tate a Tate.*"

"When the brother is a brother then the father is a father." The rich son had never bothered to even visit his poor brother, let alone help him out financially. The father was telling his rich son, when you act like a brother and help your brother, then I'll act like a father towards you.

Sholom would tell this story to explain Cain and Abel. He would say, "why didn't Hevel [Abel] cover for Kayin [Cain]? If he had said, 'Here, take my offering and give it to *Hashem*,' then he would have been a brother and *Hashem* would have acted towards them like a father. We always have to remember to cover for one another."

Sometimes Sholom would tell me about his trips abroad, and sometimes I'd have to be the one to ask him how they went. Three places he told me about stood out for him. The first was a Reform temple where the male rabbi told Sholom, "Here are the keys for the *shul*. I'm going away for the weekend with my boyfriend."

Sholom told me how everyone was sitting far away from each other. He asked them to all come closer since he couldn't use the microphone on *Shabbos* and he didn't have a strong voice. He gave the *Shabbaton* at the Reform temple and, "Since the rabbi wasn't there, I could do whatever I wanted," Sholom said with a twinkle in his eye. He retold the story about this *Shabbos* at the Reform temple so many times I lost track.

The second was a *Shabbos* he spent somewhere in the South West in America. He said he was in a real cowboy town where people still rode horses and spit tobacco. He was staying in a cheap hotel that someone from the community had arranged for him. Across the street was a saloon. He told me "it was a real saloon with real cowboys inside and horses outside."

Sholom: "I spent the whole *Shabbos* in my room. I realize now that *Hashem* put me there so I that I could go into the saloon on *Shabbos*. There was probably some Jew that I needed to meet, but I only understood that after I had left. I missed my chance."

The last was when he was invited to speak in *Chassidic* Williamsburg. Someone had arranged the talk. "They had to sneak me in the back door behind the *shul*. Then I went through a hole in the wall; literally a hole in the wall with a curtain over it."

He had such a big smile when he was telling me this (for the fourth or fifth time).

Me: "So, how did it go?"

Sholom: "They loved it. They'd never heard anything like it."

Me: "Why am I not surprised?"

O ne *Shabbos* morning after Lag BaOmer (the *yahrzeit* [anniversary of someone's death] of Rabbi Shimon bar Yochai and the 33rd day of the Counting of the Omer) I saw that Sholom had cleared a space on the bookshelves and put a full set of the Zohar with the *Mitok Midvash Kabbalistic* commentary. He told me that he bought them in Meron on Lag BaOmer.

Me: "That's very impressive. Are you planning on ever opening those books?"

Sholom: "Probably not. Everyone thinks I've read all of these books. Do you know how many books I have in this house that I've never even opened once?"

The next *Shabbos* we learned from those Zohar volumes. From that *Shabbos* on, every few weeks Sholom would open a new book that he hadn't looked at in years, or ever.

Sholom opening one of the books: "I bought this...let's see...in 1984. I still haven't opened it. Let's learn something."

I'd ask him about the rabbi who wrote the book. He always knew who everyone was and how they were related. He continued bringing new books to learn from every few *Shabboses* until our last time learning together.

S holom was very concerned about the "singles crisis" in Nachlaot (our neighborhood in Jerusalem). He once told me I should start doing *shidduchim* (setting up people on dates) in Mayanot.

Me: "Me? You should do it! Everyone thinks you're a *tzadik*."

Sholom: "I don't have time for it. I'm too busy. I wish I could find the time."

Me: "And do I have the time?"

Sholom: "Make time."

So I did. For about two years I did my best trying to help people meet each other at Mayanot. Sholom and I spoke about many of the single people we both knew. He'd ask me for information about someone and I'd ask him.

A few months before Sholom passed away, while we were learning on *Shabbos* morning we had another "*shidduch* conversation." I told him I was going to stop making an effort. Not one *shidduch* worked out. I figured I didn't have the talent for it.

Sholom: "I wish we could gather all of the single people we know, line them up—men and women—and tell them, 'you marry her, you marry him.' "

36

I n recent years I've found it hard to sleep on *Shabbos*. In the middle of the night I hear in my head, "It's *Shabbos*! How can you be sleeping?"

When I told my friends, they all said the same thing: "*Tzadikim* stay up all *Shabbos*!"

I told Sholom and he said, "That's a big *yetzer ha'ra* [evil inclination]. It won't let you sleep on *Shabbos.*"

When I would show up *Shabbos* morning for our *chevruta* exhausted from not being able to sleep he'd say, "your *yetzer ha'ra* again? Do you want a cup of coffee?"

Photo credit: Revayah Khakshouri

He Was
Someplace Else

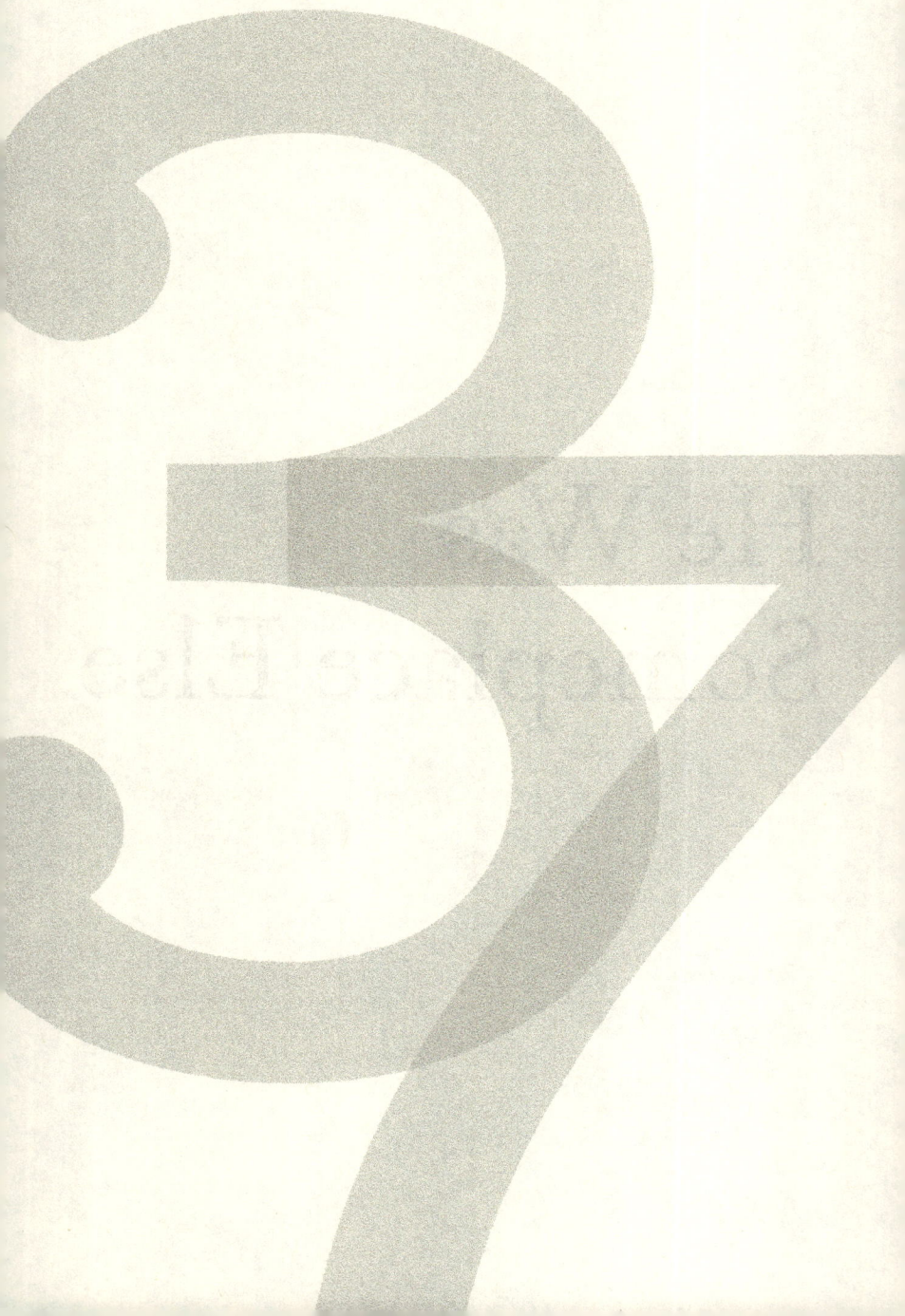

O nce when we were learning I told Sholom this thought.

Me: "We're all in *Hashem's* army. You have the infantry, those are like the Chabad *shluchim* [emissaries of the Lubavitcher Rebbe] and then you have special undercover units, like you and me."

There was total silence and he went back to the learning that I had interrupted by sharing my thought.

Me: "Don't you have anything to say?"

He was silent and then continued learning out loud.

Me: "Oh man! I hate when you do that!"

38

S holom always sang a *niggun* before each class, sometimes at the end of the class as well. Around ten years ago I told Sholom he should learn to play the guitar; maybe more people would come to the lessons. He told me he'd tried in the past, but gave up. Then he said, "Maybe you'll learn to play the guitar?"

I bought a cheap guitar and took some lessons. I volunteered myself to play a *niggun* before each class. For years I was so nervous; it could be snowing outside, but I would be dripping sweat. My fingers could not find the right chords. There was often someone in the lesson who was a great guitar player and I could see the pain on their faces when I would play the wrong chords.

Sholom, however, was very pleased. We worked together so that I would play the melodies he liked best at the pace that suited him.

When I found out he was in the hospital before he died, I came every other day with my guitar. I would play his favorite *niggunim* at the pace he liked best.

S holom would often tell this story about Rabbi Jonathan Sacks and the Lubavitcher Rebbe. Just after Rabbi Sacks received his rabbinical ordination, long before he was the Chief Rabbi of the United Kingdom and world famous, he went around to the big rebbes and rabbis and asked them what they were doing about this or that situation in the Jewish world. He was looking for a rabbi or *rebbe* to follow. He went from one *Chassidic* court to the next until he arrived at Lubavitch at 770 Ocean Parkway in Brooklyn, New York.

He asked the Rebbe what he was doing about all of the problems in the Jewish world. The Rebbe asked him, "What are you doing about it?"

Sholom would say, "You see, the Rebbe turned it around on him. Rabbi Sacks was waiting for the Rebbe to give him an answer, but the Rebbe asked Rabbi Sacks, 'What are you going to do about it?'

"Years later Rabbi Sacks wrote a long letter to the Rebbe asking if he should accept the position of the Chief Rabbi of the United Kingdom. At the end of the letter Rabbi Sacks wrote, 'Should I accept the position of Chief Rabbi?' The Rebbe answered him by putting in an editing mark to switch the words 'Should I' to 'I should.' That was the Rebbe's answer, an editorial mark! We all know what Rabbi Sacks did."

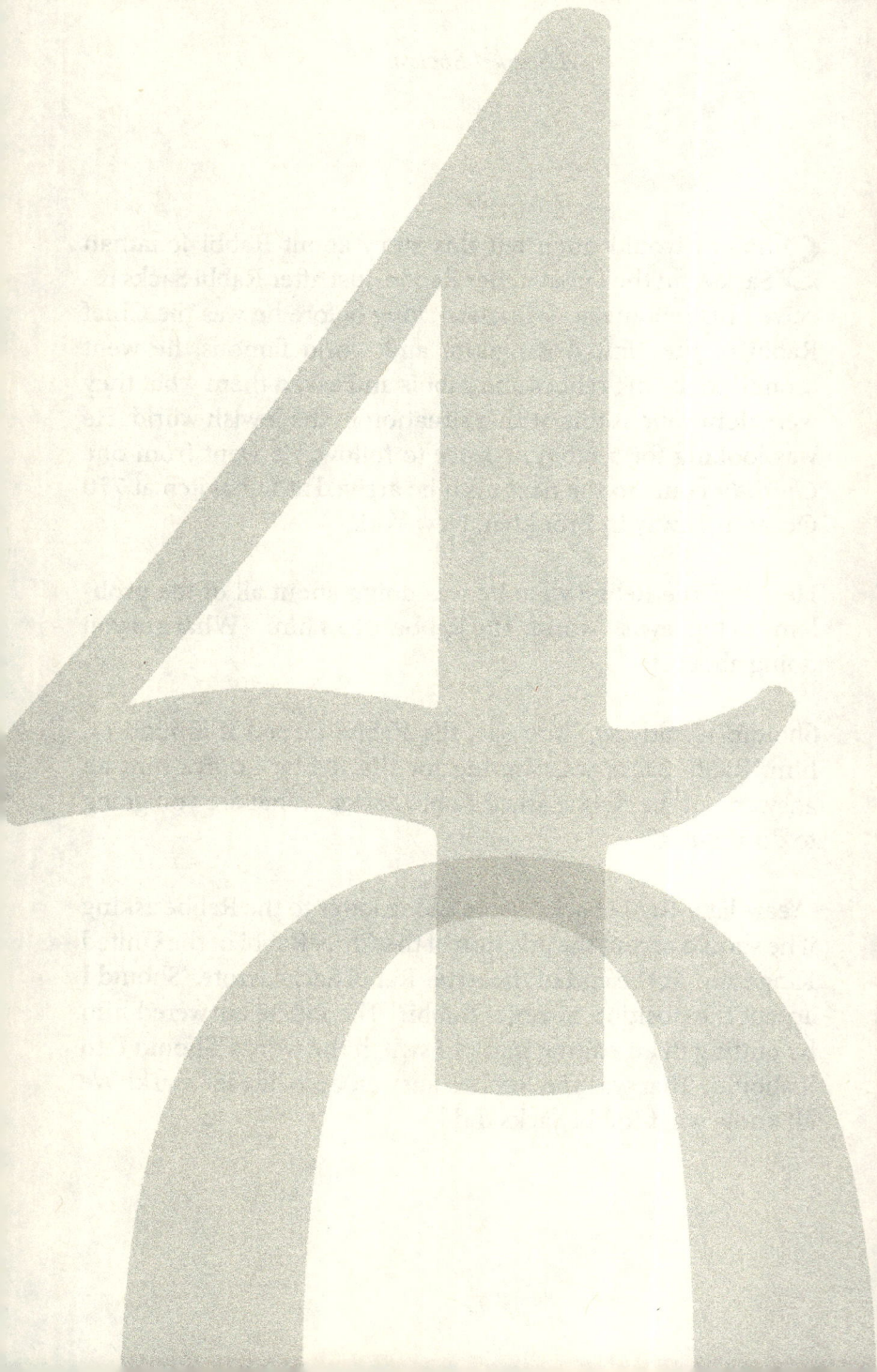

Before the "disengagement" (expulsion of the Jewish community) from Gaza, I saw a flier with the leading rabbis from each of the Orthodox Jewish communities in Israel with a picture of each rabbi and a quote on why it is forbidden to leave parts of the Land of Israel. Each of the rabbis—Litvak, Modern, Sephardic, *Chassidic*—all had untrimmed, fully grown beards. Then I saw a video of the Lubavitcher Rebbe who talked about using the counting of the Omer as an opportunity to grow a beard. I asked for my wife's permission and started growing a beard for the first time in my life during the Omer (the period between Passover and Shavuot).

I came to Sholom's Wednesday night lesson with a tiny beard. He didn't say anything. I went the full 49 days without shaving. When I came in the next week with the beard (at the point it is permitted to cut hair) he said, "Whoa! You're keeping it?" with a big smile on his face.

He never mentioned my beard again except when he told me it wasn't long enough to floss my teeth with it like he did. It actually was, but who would want to floss with their beard?

A few years after I started learning with Sholom he told me that he and Judy were going to start hosting a third meal on *Shabbos*.

Sholom: "I see that people don't have a place to go for *shalosh seudos* [third meal] and many people are not keeping the third meal. So I'm going to start giving one. I want you to come. I'll need some help."

Of course I came. The first third meal had maybe four or five people including Sholom, Judy and I. The next time was even smaller. Then Sholom started inviting everyone to the third meal. Everywhere he went he'd say, "We're hosting third meal. Please come." After the lesson on Wednesdays he'd announce, "We'll be here this *Shabbos* and we're hosting *shalosh seudos*. Please come with your friends."

Eventually people started coming. Some *Shabboses* the house was so packed you could barely squeeze in. There would be people sitting at the table and then people sitting behind them

and then people standing behind them. If we got to three rings of people around the table, it was a serious crowd.

In the beginning Sholom asked me to tell a *Chassidic* story. Eventually he stopped asking me. I asked him why.

Sholom: "You feel a part of the meal already. I want other people to feel comfortable here."

He continued asking other people to speak at the meals.

In the beginning he always insisted that I sit next to him. Sometimes at *mincha* (afternoon prayer) he would tell me to "*Daven* quickly and run back to the house to start the meal. Tell people I'll be there soon. Wash and say *hamotzei* [the blessing over bread]."

We always sang different *niggunim*. Sholom slowly figured out the ones he liked best and which ones touched the deepest places in people's souls. I don't know if he really couldn't remember Reb Levi Yitzhak's *niggun* or if it was just a way to make me feel important, but Sholom would always turn to me and say, "Reb Levi Yitzhak's *niggun*." I'd start the melody for him. There were times when I tested him. I'd tell Sholom, "You know it. Start it yourself." He'd start the Krakow *niggun* instead every time by mistake.

Eventually I moved away from the table to a corner not far from Sholom. That became my permanent spot. Sholom always made sure I ate some herring.

Sholom: "Eat the herring."

Me: "I don't like herring."

Sholom: "Eat it anyway."

I started eating one piece just so he'd leave me alone. It wasn't enough. Then he'd put two pieces on my plate and insist that I eat them while he watched. He smiled. Now I've come to like herring.

After many years I got bored with the third meal. I asked Sholom to change the *niggunim*.

Sholom: "No. That's the *seder* [order]. It's set. We're not changing it."

Me: "I'm bored with it already. How many years can we sing the same *niggunim*?"

Sholom: "What's wrong with boredom? Boredom is a good thing. You don't need to stay. Go to Rav Segal's *shul* for *shalosh seudos* if you want."

I eventually left and started going to Rav Segal's *shul*. There were times when Sholom and Judy didn't host a third meal and Sholom would join me. "I see why you like it here," he'd say.

He started *davening Maariv* (the evening prayer) at the end of the third meal, but in the first few years he didn't have a *minyan*. Since I had left for Rav Segal's meal, I always made it a habit of passing by the Brodt's house on the way home to make sure he had a *minyan*. Sometimes I was the tenth man. Sometimes, I would just stop by to wish Sholom a *"gutta voch"* (good week).

The *motzei Shabbos* (end of Shabbat) of his burial I passed by the Brodt's house hoping to see Sholom there leading the third meal, but he was someplace else.

O ne *Shabbos* morning Sholom decided to tell me about his ponchos.

Sholom: "My mother was a seamstress and my father was in the *shmata* [cloth] business. He was a strong man and would *schlep* [carry] these huge reams of cloth around. We lived in a small apartment with a couch that pulled out as our bed. During the day it was my mother's store. She would take customers and sew their clothes in that room. Sometimes she'd wake us up at night and we'd have to wait until the customer left to go back to sleep.

"I learned how to sew. I sewed this poncho myself. What do you think?"

Me: "It's very impressive. I know how to sew a little, but not like that."

Sholom: "I want to give you one of my ponchos. I have a lot of them. My kids aren't going to wear them. I want to give you one."

Me: "What am I supposed to do with it?"

Sholom with a big smile on his face: "Wear it on *Shabbos*, of course!"

Me: "Uh, okay...."

Sholom: "Come with me upstairs. I want to show you my ponchos."

He took me upstairs. There were two large cardboard cartons packed with the ponchos he'd made over the years.

Sholom: "Which one do you like?"

Me: "I don't really feel comfortable taking one. They're yours."

Sholom: "I want to give you one. Please pick one."

He took out a few and asked if I liked them.

Me: "Another time, Sholom. Maybe you'll leave me one in your will. Let's get back to learning."

He put the boxes away and we went back to learning. I told my wife, Noga, what happened.

Noga: "You should have taken one. Ask him again."

On Sunday I saw Sholom in *shul*. I told him, "I changed my mind. I'd be happy to have one of your ponchos. I'll wear it on *Shabbos*."

Sholom: "Too late."

Me: "What do you mean?"

Sholom was silent. The next *Shabbos* I asked him again for a poncho. He said, "No." I asked again and again and every time he said, "No." Eventually I let it go.

People would sometimes make a judgmental comment about Reb Shlomo Carlebach.

Sholom would say, "You are not allowed to judge a person who's not in this world to defend themselves. It's easy to judge a person who can't respond."

Me: "Are you Chabad or Carlebach?"

Sholom: "I'm a Chabadnik."

Me: "You don't look like one."

Sholom: "So what? You think Chabadnikim always wore a hat and a *kapote*? Did Reb Mendel Futerfas wear them?" (Reb Mendel was a famous Chabad *chassid* who spent fourteen years in Siberian gulags. He did not wear the traditional Chabad garb.)

Me: "So, what's the deal with Shlomo Carlebach?"

Sholom: "He was also a *Chassid* of the Lubavitcher Rebbe. Have you seen his grave?"

It says on his tombstone that Reb Shlomo was a *Chassid* of the Rebbe Rayatz.

Me: "I don't understand. Are you Chabad or Carlebach?"

Sholom: "What difference does it make?"

Then he would either tell me a story about Reb Shlomo and the Rebbe or show me a picture of them together.

S holom told me that there was a point in his life where he wanted to stop being religious. He said he kept only four Jewish things: *Shabbos, kashrut, tefillin* and *tzitziot.*

Me: "Seriously? That's called 'not being religious' for you?"

Sholom: "For me, yes. I had no oneg *Shabbos* [pleasure on *Shabbos*]. I didn't learn. My *davening* had no *chiyus* [vitality]. I was just going through the motions."

He said that during that period he went with a friend who was a rabbi to visit a big rebbe outside of Montreal. Sholom was going through a period where he wore a checkered lumberjack shirt, overalls and a cap instead of a *kippah.*

They went to visit this rebbe with Sholom dressed like a lumberjack. The rabbi and the rebbe were speaking in Yiddish. Eventually the rebbe started speaking about Sholom in front of him assuming that he didn't understand, asking the rabbi why he's hanging out with a lumberjack.

Sholom, of course, spoke Yiddish and until that point had remained silent, listening to the conversation. Sholom responded to the the rebbe in Yiddish. "I'm not a lumberjack."

The rebbe was shocked and turned to the rabbi saying, "What? The *goy* [gentile] speaks Yiddish?"

Sholom had a big smile on his face when he told me this story. "He thought I was a *goy!*"

16

Every *Shabbos* morning Sholom would ask me if I wanted a cup of coffee and some *mezonot* (cookies or crackers).

One *Shabbos* morning I told him I wasn't eating anything until after *davening* because it caused me to burp while leading the *davening*.

Sholom would always come late to *shul*. We'd go to the *mikva* together and then he'd go home to have another cup of coffee.

Eventually I started eating again on *Shabbos* morning because I was hungry. The Baal Shem Tov said to eat something before *davening* so that you eat in order to *daven* and not that you're *davening* in order to eat.

When Sholom showed up to *shul*, in the middle of my leading the *davening*, he came over and stood next to me for a while. Eventually I asked him why he was standing there.

"I'm waiting to hear you burp. When you do, make it a good one so I can hear it!" he said with a big smile.

S holom used to sit in the front of the *shul* at Mayanot. One *Shabbos* I saw him sitting in the back instead. He was there again the *Shabbos* after that one.

I asked him why he was not sitting in his regular place. He told me someone said that he thought Sholom was the rabbi of the *shul*.

Sholom told me, "I don't want anyone thinking I'm special and get some type of special privileges because they think I'm the rabbi of the *shul*."

For the next year he sat in a different seat every *Shabbos* until he felt it was safe to return again to his usual spot in the front of the *shul*.

48

S holom liked to tell this story about when he first moved to Israel. He was taking a taxi to Jerusalem from the airport and asked the driver what's the secret to living in Israel.

The driver told him, "Don't make an accounting. There will never be enough money. If your kids need bananas; buy bananas. Don't worry about it. *Hashem* will figure out where the money will come from."

Nachi (Sholom's youngest son) said, "And they were always organic bananas!"

S everal years ago a prominent Orthodox Jewish figure said they were moving to the Reform (liberal) movement.

I grew up in the Reform movement and at seventeen declared that I wanted to be a Reform rabbi. After I made my decision the first thing I did was go to a Chabad house to see what Orthodox Judaism looked like. Needless to say, I didn't become a Reform rabbi.

However, when I read this person's article I was upset. I asked Sholom what he thought. He was also upset. I told that him he should write a response. His words would carry a lot of weight.

A week later he still hadn't written anything.

Me: "Are you going to write the article?"

Sholom: "No. You write it."

Me: "Me? Why me?"

Sholom: "Because you wanted to be a Reform rabbi. You have a story to tell."

I wrote the article. Sholom read it before I published it and made a few amendments.

While Sholom was accepting of all Jews, he was not accepting of all views. He had clear red lines and opinions. He believed (as the Lubavitcher Rebbe taught) that you have to bring the people to the Torah and not the Torah to the people.

Many years ago I was deeply offended by something someone in the community had done to me personally. I wouldn't speak with him. Sholom wanted to try to work it out between us. He came to my apartment one Friday afternoon when I was cooking for *Shabbos*.

I was shocked to see Sholom at the door. "My name, Sholom, means peace. It also means a bridge. I want to be a bridge to help you make peace."

Then he gave me a hug. I was wearing an apron that was dirty from the *Shabbos* cooking and apologized to Sholom for making him dirty.

Sholom: "The *Shabbos* cooking is holy. Hug me again."

He wasn't able to solve the problem between my neighbor and me but I appreciated the visit.

One *Shabbos* morning I came for learning and was really angry.

Sholom: "What's going on?"

Me: "I'm so upset. Nothing is going right. My wife and kids are making me crazy. I was yelling at everyone on Friday afternoon and to top it all off, the *challot* [special bread for *Shabbos*] didn't rise!" (I do the *Shabbos* cooking and baking in our house.)

Sholom said calmly: "The *challot* didn't rise because you were angry."

Me: "Seriously?"

Sholom: "The *challot* didn't want to rise because you were angry."

Note to self: don't get angry until after the *challot* are baked.

When Sholom visited my office for the first time, the first thing he did was see if I had sifrey *kodesh* (Jewish books), which I did. Then he said, "Where's the *tzedakah* box?"

I showed him and he put a coin in.

One *Shabbos* I showed up and Sholom asked if I'd said the full *Shema* prayer (the *Shema* and the three paragraphs after). I told him no.

He said, "Good. Say it now. All of it. By the time we get to Mayanot it will be too late."

I did.

The next *Shabbos* he asked again.

I said it in his house again. He asked me for many months. I was already in the habit of saying it every morning. Each time he'd ask me I'd tell him I remembered. Eventually he stopped asking and never asked me again.

If you were from Canada or spoke Yiddish you were automatically Sholom's good friend, but if you were from Montreal and spoke Yiddish you were like his best friend.

I'm originally from Miami and don't speak Yiddish, so I didn't get any shortcuts.

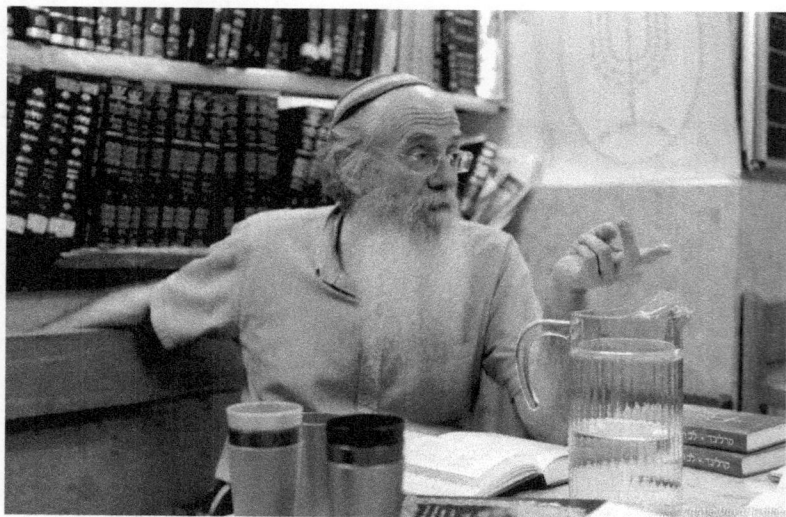

Photo credit: Jaime-David Tishler Fuks

I'll Come Visit You In Prison

I lead the *davening* daily in the Batey Rand *Shul*. Sholom once came over to me while I was leading the *davening* and told me I was saying *Kaddish* prayer too fast.

Sholom: "It's the one prayer the whole *minyan* says together besides *chazaras hashas* [repeating of the prayer out loud]. Say it slowly so we can all answer with *kavanah* [intention]."

I said it slower the next day. Sholom told me it wasn't slow enough. So, I played the game I always played with Sholom when he told me something that seemed absurd. I did exactly what he asked and exaggerated a little bit.

After saying *Kaddish* so slow I thought the *minyan* would kill me, I asked Sholom how it was.

Sholom: "That's better. Do it like that every time."

I noticed one time Sholom was leading the *minyan* after mine and said *Kaddish* quickly.

Me: "What's the deal? You told me to say *Kaddish* slowly!"

Sholom: "You're right. Thank you for the reminder. If I say it quickly again, please remind me to slow down."

In the early days of our relationship Sholom was very distant from me. It was an absolute student/teacher relationship. The friendship developed during the first few years. In those early years, sometimes I would show up at Sholom's house on *Shabbos* morning to learn with him, and either no one was home or Judy would tell me Sholom was on a trip.

I would be devastated. He wouldn't even tell me he was going away! One time, when Sholom came back, I told him that he had to tell me before he goes on a trip. He didn't understand. Then I told him how much it hurt me that he just left and didn't even tell me.

The next time he went on a trip he told me. Sometimes he would forget and call me from the States or Canada before *Shabbos*.

I'd answer the phone on Friday afternoon and it was Sholom: "Hi Barak. I'm in Montreal. I'll be back in two weeks. Have a good *Shabbos*."

That was usually the end of the conversation, but it made me so happy that he called.

When I first came to Israel I was a left winger. I voted Labor and when the left wing religious party was formed I became a member of Meimad.

I didn't speak about politics with Sholom in the first year, so I didn't know his views. One *Shabbos* morning I saw Nachi walking around the house in a Moledet youth group t-shirt. Moledet was a right of right wing party. I didn't even know they had a youth group!

I said to myself, how can I be with a rabbi who is such an extremist? But I just put it aside. Eventually, after living in Israel long enough, I stopped being a left winger, became a centrist and then over time a right winger. Sholom never criticized me for my views and never watered down his own opinions. He held firm to his views: take them or leave them.

One *Shabbos* I was learning with Sholom when my friend, Michael Avraham stopped by. Michael Avraham loves to shout "Na Nach! [a Breslover *Chassidic* slogan]"

He walked in and shouted "Na Nach!"

Sholom: "You know, people who are attracted to Chabad have big egos; Breslovers are depressed and Polisher *Chassidim*," he said with a big smile, "have problems with sexual desires."

Michael Avraham raised his eyebrows and I just smiled.

One *Shabbos* morning, while taking a *sefer* (holy book) off the shelf, Sholom turned to me and said, quoting a source I don't remember, "I learned that a teacher [i.e., rabbi] has to be careful who his students are because in *Olam Haba* [the world to come] he'll be learning with those same students for eternity."

Me: "Oy vey. No pressure, huh?"

Sholom was silent for a few seconds: "It's my honor to be your teacher."

S holom knew how to say "I don't know" when he didn't have an answer. The first time I heard him say this I was a little shocked. He's the wise sage, I thought to myself, how could he not know everything?

Over the years I enjoyed watching other people's shock when he answered, "I don't know." He taught me how to say I don't know and I'm always prepared to use it when needed.

One *Shabbos* I was spiritually flying. The next not. I asked Sholom why he thought that was. He said that *Hashem* was carrying me for one *Shabbos* and then letting me carry myself the next one.

Sholom: "*Hashem* was holding you like a child learning to walk. Then he let you go to see that you could do it by yourself. When *Hashem* lets you go, you need to learn to be even higher than when he was holding you.

"You have to allow the child to fall otherwise he'll never learn to walk. *Hashem* trusts you to fall and then get up and keep getting up until you can walk on your own."

Whenever I'd have a "down *Shabbos*" I'd try to put myself in the same mental space as the "high *Shabbos*" and eventually, after many years of doing this, my *Shabboses* got higher and higher.

I remember when *Netzach* (one of Sholom's sons) was drafted into the army. Sholom said *tehillim* (psalms) for him at every opportunity.

Me: "How do you deal with the stress?"

Sholom, rolling his eyes: "I *daven* all the time for Netzach. All the time."

He hid it well on the outside but I could see how worried he was. Then Nachi was drafted and Sholom told me he was in an elite undercover unit.

If I thought he was worried when Netzach was drafted, it was even worse with Nachi.

During one of the wars in Gaza in which Nachi served I asked Sholom how Nachi was doing.

Sholom: "He's home. Go upstairs and say 'hi' to him."

Me: "Thank God he's home. But why should I say 'hi' to him? I don't want to bother him."

Sholom: "Go say 'hi' to Nachi. I'll wait for you."

Sholom was like my commander. If he gave me an order, I followed it. I started walking upstairs. I think it was the first time I had seen that part of the house. I found Nachi's room, knocked and opened the door.

Nachi was surprised to see me.

Me: "Hi Nachi, your father asked me to come say 'hi' to you. How are you doing?"

Nachi and I had a short conversation. I told him I was happy he made it home safely and then went back downstairs to learn with Sholom. He had a big smile on his face.

L eading up to the "disengagement" (expulsion) from Gaza in 2005 Sholom would tell me at almost every opportunity how upset he was.

One *Shabbos* morning, Sholom: "What am I supposed to do? This is a disaster. It's a travesty."

I didn't know how to answer him.

Sholom got up from his chair and started slowly walking around the room.

Sholom: "What do you think would happen if I had a meeting with [Prime Minister] Sharon and punched him in the face?"

Me: "I'll come to visit you in prison."

Sholom: "I'm so frustrated. I don't know what to do!"

S holom was very interested in my kids' education. He was a teacher and principal (head teacher) for many years. When he moved to Jerusalem he was a teacher for kids in elementary school (lucky kids!). I always thought that was so brave, crazy and innocent of him to teach fifth grade in Jerusalem.

He'd always ask what's going on with my kids. One of my kids had real problems in school and was kicked out of several schools. I asked Sholom what he thought.

Sholom: "Your son is very bright. His teachers don't know how to deal with him."

When my son was kicked out of school and ended up at home for most of the school year Sholom said, "Good. He's better off at home than in that *cheder* [religious school]."

Once I asked Sholom to give me some advice based on his own kids' education.

He was silent.

Me: "What? You don't have any advice after all of these kids and all of your years of teaching?"

Sholom: "I made a lot of mistakes. Let's keep learning."

I attended Sholom's Wednesday night *parsha* class for around eighteen years. Sometimes I'd be the only person there, other times there would be twenty people there.

When there was a large crowd I'd ask Sholom what he did to increase the attendance. "I don't know where they came from," he'd say. He asked each person where they're from, and sometimes would ask how they ended up at the lesson.

There was often a burst of people before he went on one of his trips. When he got back two or three weeks later it would be down to one or two people again.

Before his last trip there was a larger crowd than usual. He said at the end, "Well, you know what this means? I must be going on a trip."

O ne *Shabbos* after going to the Skver *mikva* Sholom said he had heard there was a famous family of *chazanim* (cantors) visiting Jerusalem because their father had passed away.

Sholom: "Do you mind if we go there before we go back to learn?"

Me: "Sure. Let's go."

We walked through the neighborhood of Mea Shearim looking for a tiny *shul* where this family of cantors was *davening*. Eventually we found it. There were probably twice as many people as could fit inside. Sholom told me to be "a little *Chassidic*" and shove my way to the *bima* where the brothers were leading the *davening* in five part harmony. He told me he'd follow.

I pushed my way to the front of the *shul* making sure Sholom was behind me. We stood there watching and listening; a sight to behold.

Afterwards I asked Sholom how he knew about this.

Sholom: "Some of the guys in the *mikva* were talking about it."

Me: "You're my guide to the secret world of *Chassidic* wonder."

Sholom: "That was fun. We should do that again!"

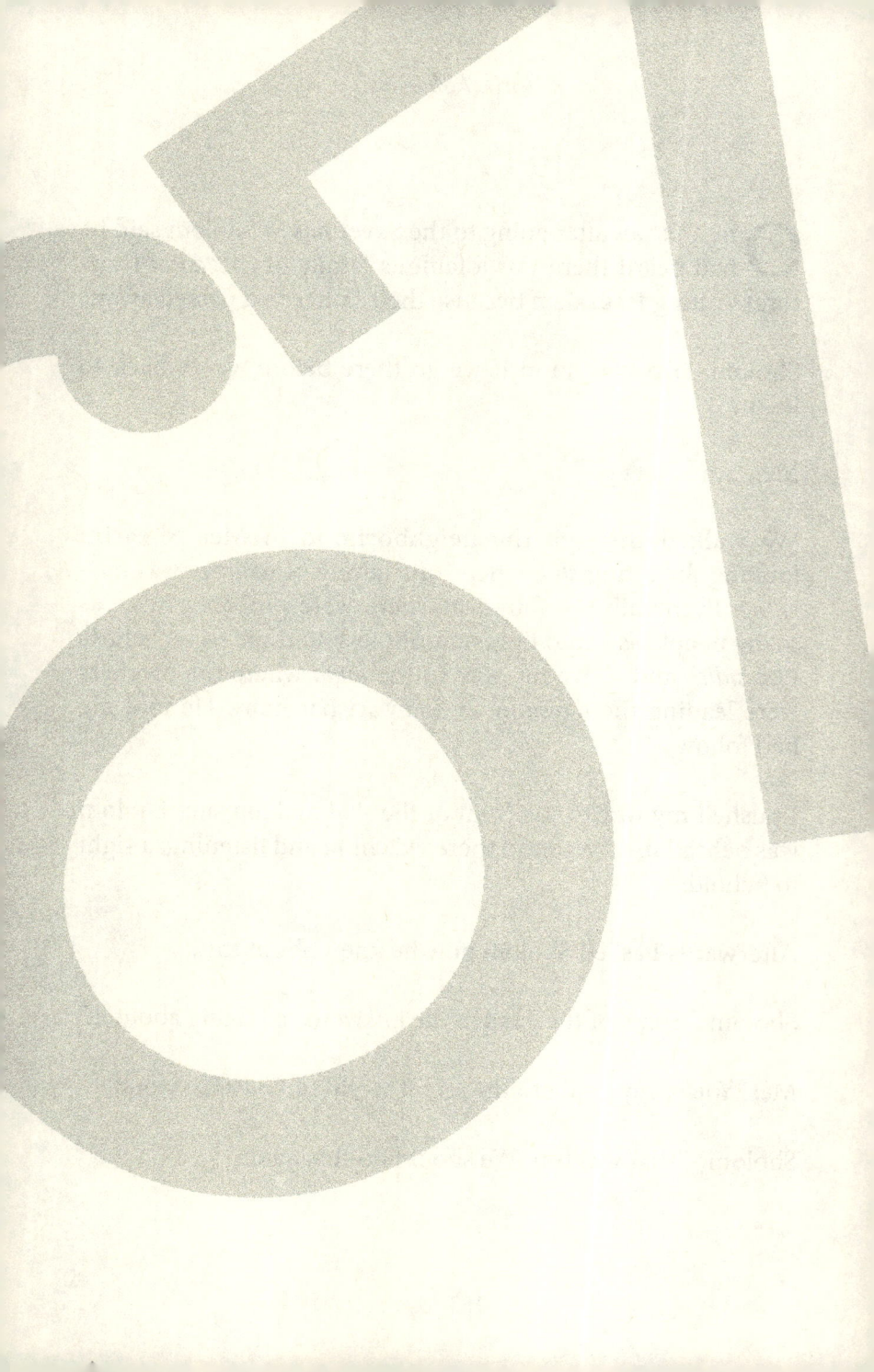

I t was like a game for Sholom to see how late he could make me for *shul* on *Shabbos* morning. I lead the *davening* every *Shabbos* morning and like to get to *shul* on time. At 8:50 every *Shabbos* morning I would interrupt Sholom in the middle of learning and tell him I had to go.

Sholom: "Wait. We're not done. Another five minutes."

I'd wait another five minutes. "Sholom, I have to leave. I'll be late."

Sholom: "Tell Shloime [Rabbi Gestetner] that I made you late. We can't just stop in the middle! A few more minutes."

We'd keep learning for another fifteen or twenty minutes. Now I was really late. I'd run to the *mikva* and then need to *daven* very quickly to catch up before I started leading *Shacharit* (the morning prayer).

Sholom would show up half an hour later and come over to me as I was singing a part of the *davening*. "Why are you *davening* so fast?" he'd say with a big smile. "Now I have to catch up!"

Then he'd turn to Rabbi Gestetner still smiling, "Was Barak late for *shul* again? We really have to do something about that."

Many times Sholom would tell me how tired he was.

Sholom: "I slept four hours last night."

Me: "That's very impressive."

Sholom: "The night before I slept two hours."

Me: "Are you taking a nap during the day?"

Sholom: "Sometimes. I have so much to do. Everyone is relying on me."

Me: "I didn't know human beings could survive on so little sleep."

Sholom: "I can't help it. Around eleven at night I get this burst of energy. I'm a night person, you know."

Me: "Ah, if only the world slept during the day and stayed up all night; you'd be set."

In the early years, I invited Sholom and Judy to come for a meal on Friday night. I was genuinely excited that Sholom would be at my *Shabbos* table. We started the meal and about ten minutes after saying *hamotzi* (the blessing for bread) Sholom put his head on the table and fell asleep. Of course I didn't want to wake him. I figured he would take a short nap, but he slept for the entire meal until Judy woke him up and told him it was time to go.

The same thing happened the second time I invited them. I asked Sholom if I was so boring that he couldn't help but falling asleep.

Sholom: "*Chas v'shalom* [God forbid]. I always fall asleep at meals, even at my own house."

S holom always used to say, "How do you know that your *davening* was good? Do you feel closer to the people you *davened* with or are you knocking people over on your way to the *kiddush* [food after *davening*]?

"If you feel closer, you know your *davening* was good. If you're rushing out of *shul* when everyone was saying *Aleinu* [the last prayer in the *davening*] then you might not need to *daven* again, but did you really *daven*?"

S holom was always going someplace or coming back from another. He'd tell me, "I was in Tzfat today. I just got back."

Me: "Tzfat? How long did it take you to get there and back?"

Sholom: "Four hours there and four hours back. I'm exhausted."

He'd make sure to be at weddings, *brises* (circumcisions), bar *mitzvahs*, concerts, lessons, army bases and anywhere else he felt that he was needed. It was a matter of principle for Sholom to "be there."

He was at every *kiddush* I ever sponsored at Mayanot, even if he *davened* somewhere else that *Shabbos*. If I told Sholom I was sponsoring a *kiddush* he'd give me a bottle of *mashkeh* (alcohol) on *Shabbos* morning and say, "This is my contribution. I'll be late but I'll be there." I always appreciated him for being there for me.

S holom was almost always tired. When he found himself unable to stay awake during his own lessons, oftentimes he would get up and teach the lesson standing.

I told him how that's a trick they use in the army. If they find you falling asleep during the day, they'll make you stand.

Sholom answered, "I can sleep standing up. I can even sleep while I'm walking. Once I went to a student's bar *mitzvah* party on a Friday night and had to walk seven miles back at night, in the snow. I was so tired I slept as I walked. Occasionally I'd sit on a bench and rest. I'm proof that you can sleep and walk at the same time. It was either that, or freeze to death, God forbid."

You Know
This Already

A few years ago one of my kids came home from school for the Chanukah vacation and told me her teacher taught that you have to use the finest quality olive oil for lighting the *menorah* (candelabra). In our house everyone lights a *chanukiah* (*menorah*) and we use olive oil. We also have a very large *menorah* outside.

After hearing this I went to the *shuk* and bought extra virgin olive oil for 55 NIS a bottle. I saw Sholom in *shul* the morning of the first day of Chanukah and told him I spent around 450 NIS buying oil for the menorahs.

Sholom: "What? Why did it cost you so much money?"

Me: "My daughter's teacher taught her that you have to use the best of the best olive oil for the *chanukiah* so I bought the best oil I could find."

Sholom: "Are you crazy? You just need an olive oil that makes a clear bright flame. Take the oil back to the store and get your money back."

Me: "Oy vey."

Sholom: "Here, take 200 NIS and go buy some cheap olive oil. You'll pay me back when you have the money."

When we'd be learning *Shabbos* morning, regardless of the time of year, Sholom would tell me to be careful not to get any crumbs in the book so that there wouldn't be any *chametz* (food forbidden) on Passover.

He was always getting ready for Passover.

S holom would always say during the Wednesday night lessons, "Barak, you know this already." I never remembered anything. I told Sholom that hopefully after twenty years of sitting in the lessons I'd start to remember something.

I still listen to his lessons every Wednesday night at 8:30 while I cook for *Shabbos*. Oftentimes I can complete his sentences, but I didn't realize it at the time when he was saying to me, "Barak, you know this already." He didn't necessarily mean that I knew it then, but when the day came that he was no longer around to guide me, I shouldn't worry because by then I would "know this already."

Once Sholom turned to me in *shul* after leading the *davening* on *Shabbos* morning and said, "I can tell that the melodies are more important to you than the words, but for other people the words are more important than the melodies."

Me: "What's more important for you: the words or melodies?"

Sholom: "The words, but I need to focus more on the melodies and you need to pay more attention to the meaning of the words. Make sure the melodies match the words."

One *Shabbos* morning Sholom turned to me and said, "What's your Cash Torah?"

Me: "What's a 'Cash Torah?' "

Sholom: "Reb Shlomo said everyone needs a Cash Torah. If you pay by check it takes a while to write out the check, but if you pay in cash it's available immediately. Everyone needs some words of Torah you can whip out at a moment's notice and share with a Jew who needs to be uplifted. Next *Shabbos*, come with a Cash Torah."

I don't know why I didn't ask Sholom what his Cash Torah was. Perhaps, since I was given a task by Sholom, I pushed everything aside and focused on my mission.

The next *Shabbos* he didn't even ask me if I had prepared my Cash Torah. So, I told him, "I have a Cash Torah."

Sholom: "Nu."

Me: "It says in the Tanya [the foundational book of Chabad *chassidus*] that every soul takes an oath before it comes into this world that you will be a *tzadik* [righteous] and not a *rasha* [evil]."

Sholom: 'That's quoting the *Gemorah* [Talmud]. Nu, keep going."

Me: "Okay, quoting the Gemorah. It says in *Tehillim* [psalms] that a *tzadik* falls seven times and gets up. So every time you fall and get back up you're fulfilling your promise to be a *tzadik* and not a rasha."

Sholom: "Did you come with that yourself?"

Me: "Yes. *Baruch Hashem.*"

Sholom: "I like that. Say it again."

Every now and then Sholom would turn to me and say, "Barak! Quick! What's your Cash Torah?"

A Shtikel Sholom

If you ever accompanied Sholom in the *mikva* you learned
that it was his personal stand up comedy club. There was
no taboo subject in the *mikva*. Unfortunately for me most of
the jokes were in Yiddish so I had no idea what everyone was
laughing about. However, as soon as we walked into the *mikva*,
regardless of which *mikva* it was, the jokes started rolling before he even started undressing.

In 2004 I travelled to the US to sell Judaica from Israel at the Reform Biennial convention. I had ordered and paid for $50,000 worth of merchandise. Much of it had been shipped to the convention, but I took whatever I could fit into my suitcases. I had borrowed a lot of the money to purchase the merchandise and the stress actually made me sick. I was sick in bed the day I was meant to leave for the States.

A few hours before I left I was still laying in bed. My wife, Noga, called me to come downstairs because Sholom and Judy had shown up at our house.

I came downstairs and saw Sholom standing at the entrance with a big smile.

Me: "What are you doing here?"

Sholom: "Judy and I wanted to wish you a safe trip; lots of *bracha* and *hatzlacha* [blessings and success]."

Me: "Thank you. I really didn't expect this."

Sholom handed me a 10 shekel coin: "Take this. You're a *shaliach mitzvah* [messenger for doing a *mitzvah*]. May you go *b'shalom* and come back *b'shalom* [in peace]."

From that point on every time I travelled Sholom gave me a coin to keep me safe, since *Hashem* gives extra protection to someone who is on a mission to do a *mitzvah*. And every time Sholom went on a trip I did the same for him.

During one Wednesday night *parsha* (Torah portion) lesson Sholom mentioned that some rabbis would *daven Shacharit, Mincha* and *Maariv* (the morning, afternoon and evening prayers) without a break in between.

He taught how you could turn the *Amida* (standing silent prayer) into a standing meditation by saying each word slowly for three seconds and pausing between the words to focus on their meaning. I've done it many times.

Sholom saw me *davening* the *Amida* for an hour and then asked me afterwards if I took his advice to turn it into a standing meditation.

Me: "Yes. And when are you going to do it?"

Sholom: "I'm too scared. I don't know what will happen to me."

Every time I asked him if he did it already he'd tell me the same thing that he was too scared. I was planning on nagging him to do it after he got out of the hospital, but unfortunately I didn't get the chance.

When I first started learning with Sholom he asked me where I *davened Shacharit* (prayed the morning prayers) during the week.

I told him most of the time I *davened* in my office by myself.

Sholom: "You have to *daven* with a *minyan*."

Me: "I need to get to work early. I don't have time."

Sholom: "I want you to go to Batey Rand. There's a *minyan* at 6:50 am. You'll *daven* there and then be at work by 8 o'clock."

Me: "Okay. But isn't Batey Rand a Yiddish speaking, *Charedi* [ultra orthodox] *shul*?"

Sholom: "Nu?"

Me: "Well I don't speak Yiddish and I'm not *Charedi*."

Sholom: "So what? You're a Jew. That's all that matters."

The first time I came to Batey Rand I felt very uncomfortable. I told Sholom and he came with me the next morning. He asked around and found me a spot in the *shul* where no one else was sitting. "This is your spot now. Sit here every day. Make this *shul* your home."

I took Sholom's advice to heart and made Batey Rand my weekday *shul*. Eventually I moved to a later *minyan* and through a strange unfolding of events ended up leading the *minyan*. At some point the *minyan* wasn't meeting on time and I complained to the *gabbai* (the person in charge).

The gabbai told me, "You're now a *gabbai*. You make sure the *minyan* starts on time."

I told Sholom that I had been made a gabbai in Batey Rand. He was shocked and entertained. In the *mikva* on *Shabbos* morning he asked the gabbai from Batey Rand if I was really a gabbai there now. When he said yes, Sholom had this look on his face like he was very pleased that I had taken his advice and made the *shul* my home.

The Cantor from the Reform temple where I grew up, came to visit me for the first time since I'd moved to Israel over twenty years earlier. It was a few weeks after Sholom had died. I told the Cantor about Sholom and he asked me, "So, what did your rabbi teach you?"

Me: "He taught me to have faith in *Hashem*, to strive to be happy, to love your fellow Jews…" and my wife, Noga, added, "…and not to take yourself too seriously."

S holom was almost always exhausted. I begged him to rest but when I did he would tell me a story about one of Rabbi Steinsaltz's (one of the great Torah sages of our time) visits to the Lubavitcher Rebbe. Rabbi Steinsaltz told the Rebbe that he had three projects each of which was a full time project and asked which one should he drop.

The Rebbe told him not only should he not drop any of them, but that he should add one more.

Sholom claimed that he didn't dream, or if he did he didn't remember any of his dreams, but sometimes he did. He told me how he had a dream once in which Rabbi Steinsaltz asked him to say the blessings under the wedding *chupah*, but none of the words would come out. Sholom took this as a sign that he wasn't doing enough, so he pushed himself to do more and more. That was his way and that's what made him happy: serving *Hashem* with every ounce of strength he had until his last days.

S holom had very high standards for himself and similar expectations of those close to him. I remember when he told me he was starting his *smicha* (rabbinical) program.

The first thing he told me was that anyone who would become a rabbi through his program had "better know how to learn a page of Gemorah or they won't get *smicha* from me. I can't stand these 'rabbis' that can't explain a page of Gemorah."

Me: "Just don't be too hard on them. Not everyone can handle you."

He brushed me off.

Sholom: "If they can't handle it, they can go somewhere else. They'd better be able to open a random page of Gemorah and explain it or I won't give them *smicha*."

Me: "Just remember to balance your high standards with some sweetness."

Sholom: "Of course, of course."

85

S holom mentioned many times a friend of his who once watched Sholom while he put on *tefillin*. This friend was a meditation master. Sholom asked him if he wanted to put on *tefillin* and the friend answered that he "could reach a higher place spiritually by meditating on *tefillin* than you [Sholom] could by putting them on."

Sholom readily admitted that this guy could reach a higher spiritual place through his meditation, but he told him that "the point is not to reach a high spiritual place. If you do that's great. The point is to put on the *tefillin*. No matter how high you reach in your meditation, you won't have done the *mitzvah* unless you actually put them on."

I once said Sholom's name to Sholom in the *mikva*. Since שלום is one of God's names you're not supposed to say it in the *mikva*. Sometimes people would shout at me not to say "Shalom" in the *mikva*. So, I would call him Shulim with a thick Yiddish accent so that no one would complain I was saying *Hashem's* name in an unclean place.

When that happened once, Sholom told me a story about a *Baal Teshuva* (someone not religious who had decided to follow Jewish law) who once came to the *mikva* and was covered with tattoos (it is forbidden by the Torah to get a tattoo). The *Charedi* guys in the *mikva* started making fun of him in Yiddish. Sholom told them, "Maybe you need to a be a little more like him and not necessarily him more like you."

He said that some people he knew who lived in the *Charedi* section of Nachlaot (our neighborhood) had told him that "in our community everything is in order [בסדר]."

Sholom asked them what they thought about their brothers and sisters in Tel Aviv. "Oy vey. Thank God we don't live there," they answered.

Sholom: "If you don't care about the Jews in Tel Aviv as much as you care about the Jews in Meah Shearim [one of the extremist religious neighborhoods in Jerusalem], then you're not בסדר." Meaning that not everything is in order in your community.

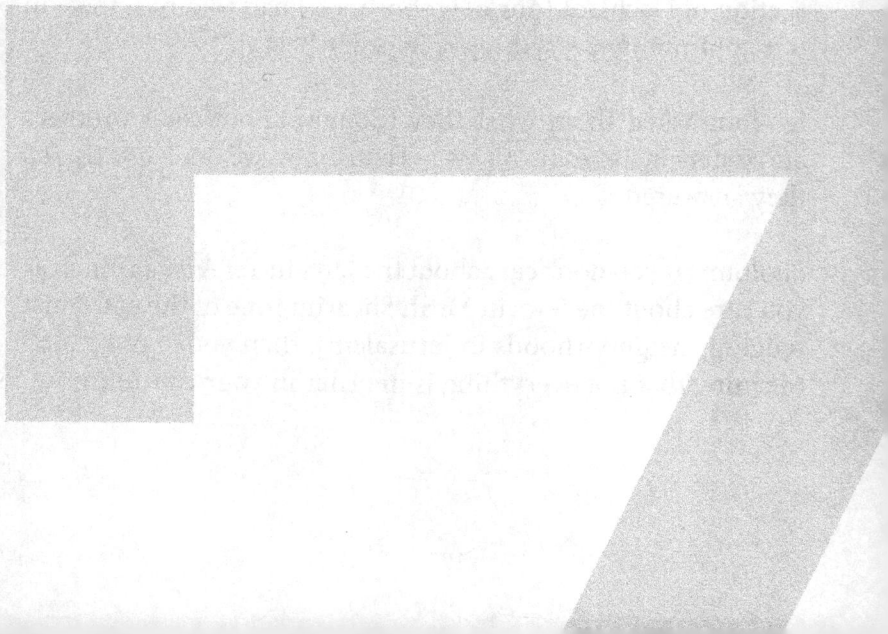

There once was a kid in the Batey Rand *shul* collecting money to buy religious books for himself to learn. The kid was fifteen years old. I gave him twenty shekels. He came to Sholom and they had a whole long conversation. Afterwards Sholom told me, "Don't give him any more money. I've arranged for him to work in the *Charedi* store in the *Shuk*. He needs to earn the money."

The next day the kid was back asking people for money again. Sholom asked him if he had shown up for the job he arranged and when the kid said "no" Sholom was upset. He told the kid there's no pride in asking for handouts when you can work. Then he said to me, "If we encourage this kid to collect money instead of working what will be of him when he becomes an adult?"

Years ago the Mayanot *Shul* split up into several smaller *shuls*. Each *shul* had its own rabbi. Sholom was upset about the split and told me "Once people respected rabbis, but now they don't. Once rabbis were revered, now most people don't take them seriously."

Once Sholom asked me if I had any debts. Unfortunately, raising a big family in Israel costs a lot of money and I had (and still have) debts. He wanted to know in detail what I had borrowed and what interest rates I was paying. After I told him he asked me to sign an agreement because he was going to lend me $1000. I told him I'd rather borrow money from the bank. I'm emotionally disconnected from the bank, but if I were to borrow money from Sholom I'd feel enormous pressure to pay it back as soon as possible.

Sholom told me: "First of all my father taught me that lending your fellow Jew interest free is one of the most important *mitzvos* anyone can do. You think I'm helping you? You're helping me!

"Secondly, you're not allowed to pressure someone to pay back the money. We'll set a schedule and you try your best to stick to it, but if you can't pay back the money right away, don't worry about it. I won't say a word. But you have to pay it back eventually! Pay off your high interest loans first. That's more important."

Eventually I paid off some of my high interest loans, but I felt a personal responsibility to pay back Sholom first. After I did he lent me the $1000 again. This went on for years. Oftentimes he would lend me more than $1000 and insist I pay off the bank and credit card loans first.

Recently a *Charedi* friend who was close to Sholom asked me, "Now that Sholom is gone who's taking care of lending money? I need a loan and would always go to him."

In the beginning I didn't enjoy the learning with Sholom. I enjoyed being around him and talking with, him but the actual learning was boring. However, I would see how excited and amazed Sholom was about what we were learning. So, I started asking him, "What's so amazing? Why are you so excited?" He would explain to me what he had assumed I understood and was also amazed by. Slowly I came to understand Sholom's method of understanding *Chassidus* and at times he would ask me to explain to him what I was so excited about; what I found so amazing in the text.

Photo credit: Shmuel Diamond

What Are the Three Words You Always Hear When You Enter a New Shul?

This was one of Sholom's classic lessons that he repeated again and again. The word *mitzvah*, which means commandment, comes from the same Hebrew root as "tzvat" which are pliers. What's the connection between a commandment from God and pliers? Pliers bring two ends, two extremes, together. When the pliers are fully open, the two ends are far from each other, but when you close the pliers the two ends are as close as they could be; still separate but ultimately part of the same tool. That's what a *mitzvah* does for our relationship with *Hashem*.

Hashem is infinite. We are finite. How is it possible for the finite to reach the infinite? It's impossible. Every time the finite would come closer to the infinite, the infinite would always be further away. The only way is for the infinite to come close to the finite; that is for *Hashem* to come close to us. And how does He do that? Through the *mitzvot*.

Abraham Joshua Heschel said that when we do a *mitzvah*, we "do what *Hashem* is." The *mitzvot* allow us to connect with *Hashem* because *Hashem* (the infinite) is reaching out to us. When we do a *mitzvah*, we create a bond with *Hashem* even though the distance between us and God would be infinite if it were not for the *mitzvot*.

S holom said Rebbe Nachman taught that sometimes when we're learning we have to stop for a minute and say a prayer that we'll merit to remember whose teachings we're learning from; that what we're learning is from *Hashem*.

S holom had once helped me with some tax issues I was having by referring me to an accountant he trusted and used. She was very good and solved my problems. I continued using her services for many years.

Then she got sick. She continued working from her hospital bed literally until her last day, helping as many people as she could before she left this world.

We went to visit her in the hospital.

Sholom warned me that we were going to see a lot of people in really bad shape.

I told him it didn't bother me. I had wanted to be a surgeon when I was a kid and used to watch surgeries on the The Learning Channel.

When we came in I could see death on our accountant's face. She was trying to smile and was still on the phone giving people tax advice.

We spoke with her for a little while. Then wished her good health and left. We went home on the bus in silence.

A couple of days later I asked Sholom how the accountant was doing.

"She died the night we came to visit her."

Me: "Oh my God. *Baruch Dayan HaEmet* [blessed is the true judge]. When's the *levaya* [funeral]?"

Sholom: "It was yesterday."

Me: "Why didn't you tell me?"

Sholom: "It doesn't matter now."

Me: "You have to tell me things like this. I wanted to be at the *levaya*."

Sholom: "You're right. I should have told you."

S holom mentioned many times that in the Chabad *Siddur* just before *davening* we say, הריני מקבל עלי מצות עשה של ואהבת לרעך כמוך "I accept upon myself the *mitzvah* of loving my fellow Jew."

He would say, "What are the three words you always hear when you enter a new *shul*?

"That's my seat."

Sholom would say, "It's fine to have a permanent seat in *shul*, but when someone new comes and sits next to you make sure you say to them '*Sholom aleichem*' [the traditional Jewish greeting of 'peace be upon you'] to fulfill the obligation that you took upon yourself of loving your fellow Jew."

As a result, I have said good morning and introduced myself to many of the people that sat next to me in *shul*. Sometimes I do it on the first day; sometimes it takes me a couple of days, but thanks to Sholom I've made many friends in *shul*. Even if I never see these Jews again, at least I made them smile that morning by saying '*Sholom aleichem*' to them in *shul*.

Around 2011, Sholom started broadcasting videos of his lessons on YouTube. At first it was a bit strange. I was used to the intimate lessons; there was something special in knowing they were just a moment in time.

I once asked Sholom why he was broadcasting and recording these videos.

Sholom's answer was simple, "Maybe someone will watch them one day."

Every now and then Sholom would call me Friday just before *Shabbos*. Sometimes it would be to tell me that he and Judy were going away for *Shabbos* and not to come by *Shabbos* morning. But sometimes he would call just to wish me a good *Shabbos*. I thought it was so strange. Why would he call me to wish me a good *Shabbos* when I'd see him at Mayanot in a couple of hours?

Occasionally I got a text message from him just before *Shabbos*, "have a wonderful *gutten Shabbos kodesh* [good holy Shabbat]."

I didn't understand it until I asked him one time when he called me. "Why are you calling to wish me a good *Shabbos* when I'll see you in a few hours?"

Sholom: "Reb Shlomo would collect numbers of people all around the world and call them. I try to do the same before *Shabbos*. I was calling and texting people and I thought you might also like me to call you and wish you a good *Shabbos*."

Me: "I do. Thank you for calling me. *A gutten erev Shabbos*."

Somehow Sholom was always able to speak with children on their level. He knew what questions to ask them and how to make them laugh. It was a talent I've never seen in anyone else.

I once asked him, "Sholom, how do you know to say exactly the right things to little kids?"

Sholom: "I was a teacher for many years."

Me: "No. It's more than that. You have a unique talent for this."

Sholom rolled his eyes.

Me: "Nu. Seriously."

Sholom: "I guess what they want to hear and tell them."

S ometimes people came to Sholom and asked for a *bracha* (blessing). If it was a simple blessing he would just say, "*Hashem*, please give [this person] a *shidduch* [a match]," livelihood, children or whatever else the person asked for.

But sometimes people would treat Sholom like a rebbe; coming over with their heads bowed down, kiss his hand and insist on a *bracha*.

It happened many times that I was with him when someone treated him like a rebbe. He'd point to me with a big smile on his face and say, "Ask him for a *bracha*. He's the real *tzadik*."

My answer was always the same, "Look at the two of us. Which one of us looks like a *tzadik*? Me or him?" I'd say pointing back at Sholom.

Inevitably, the person would go back to Sholom and ask for a blessing. Then I would answer amen.

I always sponsor the *kiddush* at Mayanot on Passover and Sukkot because no one else would bother. For Sukkot I used to build the *sukkah* myself (now there's a permanent structure for the sukkah) so we would have a place to have the *kiddush*. For Passover I have to buy everything and make sure it has a very strict *hechsher* (kosher certificate). I forgot to buy water with a special Passover *hechsher*. I asked Sholom on *Shabbos* morning if he thought it was a big deal.

Sholom: "Why would anyone need a *hechsher* on water? Do you also need one on air? It's just a way to make money. It's absurd, and idiotic."

Some people refused to drink the water at the *kiddush* because it didn't have a Passover *hechsher*. Sholom poured the water in front of everyone, drank it and told them that "Water doesn't need a *hechsher*."

The next year I made sure to buy water with a Passover *hechsher*.

Sholom: "Why did you bother? You don't need it."

Me: "What do I care? It costs the same price to buy the brand of water with the *hechsher* as it does to buy the one without it."

Sholom: "You see! It's all about business. You don't need a *hechsher* on water."

At the *kiddush* I gave Sholom a bottle that I bought for him without a *hechsher*. It was worth it just to see the smile on his face.

I had to really invest in my relationship with Sholom. I thought that he was a certain personality, but then when I got closer to him I discovered someone different.

There were many times when friends would come away from a meeting with Sholom confused because they didn't expect him to be so harsh with them. There were times when I would come home and tell my wife, "What do I need this for? Sholom is nuts! I can't take him."

I came to learn that there were three levels of Sholom. The first was the sweet, hippie rabbi that smiled, joked and always gave an encouraging word and accepted everyone unconditionally.

The second was a very strict, harsh person who had extremely high standards for himself and those who were close to him.

The third was the true sweet, caring person under the first two layers. When you reached that place, it was like you finally found what you were looking for in Sholom. He was strict, caring and encouraging all at the same time, but you had to have a lot of patience and persistence to get there. It wasn't easy for me, but I'm glad I stuck it out.

S *habbos* morning was my time to share with Sholom anything that was on my mind. Sometimes I would save it for the walk to the *mikva*, other times I would just lay it on him after he finished saying the morning blessings.

I'd spend five minutes or so telling Sholom about my kids or something that was bothering me and he wouldn't even look at me. He was just silent.

Me: "Sholom, are you okay?"

Sholom: "*Baruch Hashem*."

Then he wouldn't say anything else. We would just sit there in silence. There were times when I would push him to talk and answer me but many times I just sat there with him in silence. Sometimes we'd simply walk to the *mikva* in silence as well.

I made it into a game where I would wait until Sholom spoke before I said another word. Often the silence was either broken with Sholom saying "Let's learn" or a joke. I learned to accept these periods as a kind of silent meditation.

Sholom had a phenomenal memory and could quote by heart verses from all kinds of Jewish books; old and new. Sometimes he'd doubt himself as to whether he remembered the correct source or quoted it correctly. "Let's look it up," he'd say and almost every time he remembered not only the book, but also the page and where on the page to find it.

S holom would tell this story about Moish Geller and Judy.

Judy had a meeting with a realtor in the *Shuk* at 1:15 pm. She had left the house early but the realtor wasn't in his office so she went back home. A few minutes later Judy was just on her way out again when Moish Geller stopped by the house.

"Judy, I need a cup of coffee."

Judy was about to lock the front door. "Moish, I can't now. I have a meeting in the *shuk*. I have to go."

Moish wouldn't take no for an answer. He insisted. Judy obliged.

"Drink fast, Moish. I have a meeting I'm already late for."

Moish appreciating the favor, "Judy, you're *mamash* saving my life with this cup of coffee. You have no idea, holy sister."

When Moish finished the coffee. Judy ran to the meeting. Now she was late. On the way she heard a loud explosion. There was smoke and debris flying in the in air. People were screaming in a panic.

She called the realtor. "Don't come! Don't come. Everything happened right here!"

Reb Shlomo would always thank someone by saying, "You're mamash saving my life."

Sholom concluded, "Moish thought Judy was saving his life by giving him a cup of coffee, but actually Moish saved Judy's life."

S holom and I were in *shul* once when someone was leading the *davening* with a great deal of energy. I call this guy "the Bulldozer" since his *davening* is so forceful it was like being run over by a bulldozer.

I asked Sholom what he thought of the Bulldozer's *davening*.

Sholom: "He needs to add some sweetness to his *davening*."

S holom told me that he was starting a *smicha* (rabbinical) program.

Me: "What do you need that for?"

Sholom: "What do I need any of this for? I didn't want to open a yeshiva! That was Shlomo's dream. But people gave me money and pushed me to open the yeshiva.

"Do you think I want to run a *smicha* program? *Hashem* isn't giving me a choice. He's forcing me to do this. I just have to accept it and do it to the best of my ability."

Afterwards, though, he had a big smile on his face because Sholom knew he was doing what *Hashem* created him for.

At Sholom's funeral I was sitting in the van with the body. Someone started singing the Poltava Rav's *niggun* (which was one of Sholom's favorite melodies, that he would sing every third meal).

In general Sholom was strict about singing *niggunim* (melodies) precisely, especially Reb Shlomo's *niggunim*.

The Poltava Rav's *niggun* is a little complicated and even Sholom himself made mistakes until I found a recording of it online and we learned it together.

Whenever we'd be singing together at a *farbrengen* (*Chassidic* gathering) or at a lesson and someone would sing the melody incorrectly, Sholom would stop everyone, correct the mistake and continue. He'd do this as many times as was needed until we sang it correctly.

During the funeral somehow everyone made the mistake that always made Sholom stop the *niggun* in the middle, correct everyone and keep going. I was sure he was going to lift his head from the stretcher, shout at us to sing it correctly and then lay back down.

But if he did that people might think he was a *tzadik*, so he didn't.

Sholom taught that "the most God-like thing you possess is the ability to make decisions. You can make a decision to change your nature. Animals can't do that. You can make a decision to keep *Shabbos* and you can keep *Shabbos*. It may not be easy, but if you're a tough person once you make a decision you'll stick with it."

This was another one of Sholom's classic lessons that he would give over at least once a year.

It says in the Torah (Deuteronomy 4:2) that you may not add or subtract anything from it. Sholom was once a tutor for a girl whose father was a "gangster," Sholom would say with a big smile and a laugh. "No, really. He was a gangster with guns at home. He even served time in prison, I think."

They were learning this lesson and to make the point Sholom pointed to an original Picasso painting they had hanging on the wall in their house.

("You see," Sholom would say, "I told you he was a real gangster!")

Sholom took a marker and went over to the Picasso, asking the girl, "What would happen if I made a little change to this painting?"

The girl responded, "My father will kill you."

Sholom, smiling: "And she meant it!"

He asked the girl, "What would happen if I just scraped away a little bit of the painting here in the corner where no one will notice?"

The girl saying slowly: "My father will kill you."

Sholom: "So, you see, if it's such a big deal to make a little change on a painting from some famous artist, all the more so for the Torah that was given to us directly from God."

Now The Little Lights Will Shine Brighter

Occasionally Sholom would give me a *sefer* (a religious book) as a gift. I always insisted that he write a dedication in the front of the book. He always wrote them in Hebrew. The image below is from a set of books we used to learn from on *Shabbos* morning taken from *sichos* (talks) of the Lubavitcher Rebbe.

Here's the translation:

To our dear friend, beloved and loyal, Abba Barak ben Kalman DovBer may his light shine, with joy always, with blessings for great success physically and spiritually together with all of the members of your household with love and blessings, Sholom

M any times I would come on *Shabbos* morning and Sholom and Judy would still be asleep.

Sholom had told me to knock on the door and shout, "*Gut Shabbos*! Sholom! Wake up!" until he woke up. Sometimes I would have to knock for ten minutes or more. I didn't want to wake up the neighbors. So, one *Shabbos* I found a stone on the ground and gently tossed it up to the bedroom window.

It worked. Sholom opened the window and told me, "Go to the *mikva* and come right back."

When I got back Sholom told me that the stone I threw at the window was *muktzeh* (an object that can't be used on *Shabbos*) unless I had designated it before *Shabbos* to be used on *Shabbos*.

The next *Shabbos* I used one of the wood boards from their Sukkah to bang on the window and wake up Sholom. He told me that the wood board was also muktzeh unless I had designated it to be used on *Shabbos* before *Shabbos*.

After that I had a small pile of stones in their courtyard that I had officially designated for *Shabbos*. I showed it to Sholom at the Wednesday night lesson and told him these were my stones for waking him up on *Shabbos*. He didn't say anything on *Shabbos* morning.

I tossed the stones at the window until Sholom or Judy woke up. I was very pleased that it worked and I didn't violate *Shabbos* this time.

Sholom: "Please just knock on the door until we wake up. I don't want you to break the window."

Me: 'I don't like shouting so early in the morning. I don't want to wake up the neighbors."

Sholom: "How do you know the neighbors don't want you to wake them up? They also have to get to *shul* and *daven*. Knock hard until I get up."

I always admired Sholom and Judy's relationship. It was a quiet, private love; a relationship of mutual respect and admiration.

Sholom always said at the lessons that Judy was a *tzadeket* (a righteous woman) and the real force behind the yeshiva, the third meal, and the person he had become.

He told the story of how they came to Israel for the year and when the year ended Judy wished Sholom a safe trip back to Montreal. She was staying. He went back to work for a year and then moved to Jerusalem where Judy and their children were waiting for him.

During the third meals Judy would sit at the back of the room and make hand motions signaling to Sholom—who always spoke softly with his voice gradually getting softer and softer the longer he spoke—to speak louder since half of the room couldn't hear him. Sholom would see Judy signaling to him and ask, "Can you hear me in the back?" Judy would shout back, "No!" with a big smile on her face.

The Brodt's house is always filled with fresh flowers. Once Judy was away and I saw Sholom taking care of the flowers.

Me: "What's going on? Are you a florist now?"

Sholom: "I promised Judy I would take care of the flowers. Some of them died and I'm replacing them. I learned from Judy the healing power of beauty. I never understood it until I met Judy."

Sholom was very proud of Judy's work as a birth coach and interior designer. Whenever she would assist with a birth he would wish me a *mazal tov* (congratulations) since "another Jewish baby has come into the world."

One story he would tell often was this: after Judy assisted a woman with a birth in Tzfat she ran into someone on the street who asked her where she could find a deep spiritual experience or a good lesson.

Judy answered, "If you want a deep spiritual experience there's a woman who just gave birth. Go help her wash her dishes and fold laundry."

Whenever Sholom would repeat this story in the lessons he'd say, "Barak has a big family with lots of dishes to wash and clothes to fold. Whoever goes and helps him and his wife, I assure you, will have a deep spiritual experience."

On *Shabbos* morning Sholom would make a cup of coffee for himself. By the time Judy would come down he had finished his first cup. Either he would ask Judy to please get him another cup of coffee or Judy would bring him one before he even asked. Sometimes she would bring him tea instead telling him it was healthier.

I remember how every *Shabbos* morning Sholom would put rice milk in his coffee. He'd look at me with a big smile and ask, "Do you have normal milk in your house? This rice milk doesn't blend into the coffee. It just sinks to the bottom. But that's what Judy likes, so I drink it."

Judy was always taking care of Sholom and Sholom did his best to always take care of Judy. Rebbe Nachman says that you can learn from the everyday actions of a *tzadik*: how he gets dressed, how he interacts with vendors in the market, how he folds his tallis. I learned so much just by watching the beautiful relationship between Sholom and Judy. They were blessed to have one another and I was blessed to learn from them by being in their presence for so many years.

People have asked me what Sholom and I learned together on *Shabbos* mornings. The short answer is the well-known joke, "Where does an 800 pound gorilla sit? Wherever he likes." What did we learn? Whatever Sholom wanted.

For the first few years we learned *sichos* (talks) of the Lubavitcher Rebbe translated by Rabbi Sacks in the book *Torah Studies*.

We studied that book together for three years, repeating it each year. I would read out loud in English while Sholom followed along in the original Yiddish. After I read each paragraph he'd ask me to explain it and if I didn't understand it, he'd tell me to read it again. "This time pay attention to what you're reading," he'd say.

Then we moved on to learning from *Chassidus Mevueres* which are lessons from the Alter Rebbe (the first Chabad rebbe). These Sholom would read and translate while I listened and asked questions. We pretty much stuck with Chabad *Chassidus*. Sometimes we would learn from the Alter Rebbe's *Shulchan Aruch* (book of Jewish law), especially if a holiday was coming up. And, of course, on every holiday we would learn from Reb Shlomo.

After Sholom died many people asked to learn with me on *Shabbos* morning, but I turned them all down. (I still learn on my own before the *mikva* and then at 8:15 with Rabbi Gestetner on *Shabbos* morning.) I told them, "I didn't go to Sholom for the learning. That I could find in many other places. I went to Sholom because of Sholom. There's no replacing him for me."

S holom (and his brother) were second generation survivors of the Holocaust since his parents were survivors. He would often mention his father's children who perished at the hands of the Nazis.

He thought as a kid that part of being Jewish was not having grandparents. None of the kids in his class in his *cheder* had grandparents since they all died in the War. He told me how shocked he was when he met a Jewish kid that had grandparents.

I grew up on Miami Beach with so many Holocaust survivors that I thought that every older Jew had to have a tattoo on their arm to be Jewish. But I also grew up with all four of my grandparents. Sholom always told me to cherish my relationship with them. He wished he had known what it was like to have his own grandparents in his life.

Sholom once told me about a couple he knew back in Montreal. The wife was a convert and the husband born a Jew. She had an Orthodox conversion.

The couple got divorced and she went back to being a Christian.

Sholom: "I'm very concerned for her. I helped her with her conversion."

Me: "What are you concerned about? They're divorced now."

Sholom: "She had an Orthodox conversion. If she stops being Jewish, it's a matter of life and death. I'm very concerned about her."

I remember several people that we knew who had Orthodox conversions where Sholom would say to me, "I hope he understands what he's doing in becoming a Jew. He can't go back. Once he converts that's it. He's a Jew for life. It's a matter of life and death."

15

I attended Sholom's *parsha* lesson on Wednesday nights. I
remember telling him at some point that I thought it was
strange to be preparing for *Shabbos* on Wednesday night since
I rarely thought about *Shabbos* until Friday morning.

Sholom showed me in the *davening* for Wednesday that there's
the verse from the Friday night *davening*, "*L'chu l'ran'na.*"

"That was put there as a reminder to prepare for *Shabbos.*"
He also said that the latest time you can make *havdalah* (the
blessing after *Shabbos* is over) is on Tuesday. That teaches us
that we continue to get the energy from the past *Shabbos* until
Tuesday night and then from Wednesday we're already getting
the energy from the next *Shabbos*.

So the earliest time to prepare for the next *Shabbos* is on
Tuesday night. By the time we got to Wednesday night, we
were well into the preparation time for *Shabbos*.

I started getting ready for *Shabbos* on Wednesday by inviting
guests, planning the menu, buying some of the food for *Shabbos*
and, of course, attending Sholom's class.

Then I started getting ready on Tuesday night and, eventually,
as soon as *Shabbos* ended on Saturday night I would start
getting ready for the next *Shabbos*. It was at that point that I
realized Sholom long ago had been getting ready for *Shabbos*
all week long and by the time the Wednesday night lesson
came along he was already well into the upcoming *Shabbos*.

I had to train myself to stay awake during Sholom's lessons. He himself was usually exhausted and would fall asleep at times during his own lessons. Then on top of it he spoke softly and calmly. One of my tricks was to ask as many questions as I could, especially ones that would throw Sholom off. That way we'd both stay awake.

I would also make jokes in my head and occasionally share them with Sholom and the class. At first I was worried that he would be annoyed with me; asking provocative questions and telling jokes. But once Sholom thanked me for the jokes and questions; telling me that it clarified the lesson for others, and, with a smile, "also kept them from falling asleep."

Many times Sholom and I would have conversations on *Shabbos* either before our learning or in the middle. I would share my problems and thoughts with Sholom and he would share his with me, whenever I could get him to open up and talk.

Oftentimes we would be talking about something like my children's education and then Sholom would say, "Let's start learning" and open up a *sichah* (talk) of the Lubavitcher Rebbe. In the first paragraph the Rebbe would talk about the exact problem I was having with my children's education; the same problem that Sholom and I had been talking about a few minutes before.

It wasn't just with the Lubavitcher Rebbe, this would happen with many different rebbes and even with the *Shulchan Aruch.*

I found it astonishing. Every time I'd say to Sholom, "Don't you think it's amazing that we were just talking about this right now and here it shows up in our learning?"

Sholom's answer was always the same: "So."

Me: "So? How can you say 'so?' "

Sholom: "It happens to me all the time."

S holom spent a lot of time trying to save marriages. There was a period when practically every time I came by the Brodt's house there was another couple in their kitchen or his office. He'd ask me to wait in the other room until he finished, but sometimes I could overhear the conversations.

When we'd get together I would ask Sholom what was going on.

Sholom: "So many couples just can't seem to get it together. He won't listen to me and she won't listen to me either."

Me: "What do you say to them? How do you know what to say?"

Sholom: "Whatever seems right at the time. I don't have any set lines or parables. I listen to them and try to help. I don't know if it makes any difference, but at least I'm trying. It says in the Gemorah that the *mizbeach* [the altar in the Temple] cried when a couple got divorced. I'm trying to spare the couple and *Hashem* that pain. I know what it is to be divorced. I was deeply depressed after my divorce."

Years later I noticed fewer couples when I would come by the house. I asked Sholom if this was just because he was meeting them at different times and I missed them?

Sholom: "I'm spending less time trying to help couples. If they come to me, I'll do my best. I have other things I need to do and limited time and energy. I have to focus my efforts on the yeshiva. It takes so much work."

I once shared with Sholom and Judy on a *Shabbos* morning my 2 step method for getting married and 1 step for staying married.

To get married you need: 1) to be attracted to the person and respect them, and 2) to have common goals for yourselves and how you want to raise your children.

To stay married you need to always strive to see the good in your spouse and accept them as they are. Don't expect them to change. If they change for the better, that's great, but what you married is what you get. The more you can accept and appreciate your spouse, the longer you'll be married.

Sholom gave me a "pssshh" and Judy said, "How does it feel to be so wise?"

I wasn't sure if she was being serious, sarcastic or maybe both.

120

A Shtikel Sholom

S holom always led the Musaf prayer at Mayanot on the *Shabbos* closest to his father's *yahrzeit*. He wanted to sing Carlebach melodies with the *davening*. Sholom would ask me to stand next to him to give him support just in case he got nervous and couldn't remember the melodies.

I loved standing next to Sholom as he led the *davening* but I didn't really believe he needed my help. I'd stand there and let him start the melody.

He often forgot how it went, even melodies that he knew well. Sholom would turn to me and signal that he needed my help. I'd start singing and then he'd remember it right away. Afterwards he'd say "Thank you for saving my life."

267

In my first few meetings with Sholom I told him how I felt that now that the Lubavitcher Rebbe and Reb Shlomo had passed away there were no revealed great Jewish leaders like them anymore. I asked Sholom what he thought.

Sholom: "They were big lights. Now the little lights will shine brighter."

Me: "I don't understand."

Sholom: "Imagine you're in a football stadium. All of the lights are on. You can see everything. But what if the lights are turned off and now it's pitch black? If you light a candle, you'd see it from anywhere in the stadium because even though the light is small, the darkness is so great that the little light shines brighter."

Me: "So, you're the little light in the darkness?"

Sholom: "I'm one of them and so you are you."

Years ago I read a couple of books on Jewish humor. I picked out some of my favorite jokes and told them to Sholom. He didn't even pretend that he hadn't heard the jokes before, he simply finished each one after I gave him the first few words. I tried for weeks to stump him, but he knew every joke in the book. Then he'd tell me jokes that weren't in the books I read. I forgot most of them, but here's one that I remember.

A Jewish kid in Russia is asked, "Who is your father?"

"Lenin!"

"Who is your mother?"

"Mother Russia!"

"What do you want to be when you grow up?"

"An orphan!"

Here's a joke of Sholom's that Yisrael Smith shared:

This guy walks into a bar with a chihuahua. The bartender says to him "Hey, we don't allow dogs in here!"

The guy says "Oh, it's OK, this is my seeing-eye dog."

The bartender says "You have a chihuahua for a seeing-eye dog?"

The guy says "They gave me a chihuahua?!"

O ne Friday afternoon Sholom called me. I answered the phone with "*Gut erev Shabbos*" which I learned to do from Judy.

Sholom: "Barak, you're taking another guest for *Shabbos*. My friend Rabbi Poupko needs a place to eat."

Me: "How do you know I have more room for guests?"

Sholom: "You'll make room."

Me: "Yes, sir. I'll take care of your friend."

Rabbi Poupko suddenly passed away a few months after Sholom. Sholom and Rabbi Poupko were *chevrutas* (learning partners). Here are some short stories about Rabbi Poupko.

When I first met Rabbi Poupko I introduced myself and asked him what was his name. "Rabbi Poupko" was his answer.

Me: "What's your first name?" I don't like to call people by the title rabbi unless they insist.

Rabbi Poupko: "Rabbi. You just call me Rabbi. Okay?"

Me: "Boy, it must have been hard on you as a kid growing up with the first name Rabbi."

Rabbi Poupko: "My name is Yaakov Moshe. You can call me Yaakov Moshe if you want."

Rabbi Poupko was a Torah genius. He could quote any passage from major and minor Jewish texts by heart. I once asked him if he had a photographic memory. He told me that he did not, but that he had made a conscious decision to memorize what he learned and repeat it often.

Me: "If that's the case, you must be repeating Torah all the time in your head."

Smiling Rabbi Poupko answered: "Something like that."

Rabbi Poupko was extroverted in public but inside he was an introvert. He was somewhat socially awkward, but his distinguished presence compensated for it. I remember one *Simchat Torah* when Rabbi Poupko was at Mayanot at night.

He didn't feel comfortable enough to participate in the dancing, so he planted himself right in the center of the action at the *bima*. People all around Rabbi Poupko were dancing, a bit drunk, singing at the top of their lungs and banging on the *bima*. And there was Rabbi Poupko holding onto the *bima* with his eyes open deep in concentration, taking in the powerful energy around him.

He did this in subsequent years as well. I always admired Rabbi Poupko for this. He could have just stayed on the side, but he put himself right in the middle of the action and took it all in. I thought to myself, that's a man who knows who he is and what he needs.

Rabbi Poupko had a regular slot at the Mayanot *kiddush* where he would give over a *d'var Torah* that was so intellectually rich I usually didn't understand it. If he was inspired he'd tell us a *Chassidic* story or a story from his youth. Everyone at the *kiddush* would ask Rabbi Poupko where were his books. He was so brilliant and expressive how come he hadn't published multiple books already?

His answer was always the same, "In the academic world they have a phrase 'publish or perish.' However, I say it like this, 'perish then publish.' I have all of my writings on a hard drive. My family knows where to find them. After I die, they'll publish my books."

The first thought I had after I heard that Rabbi Poupko had passed away was that his books would finally be published.

Rabbi Poupko and I became good friends over the years. I really appreciated when he opened up to me and shared his problems with me. I came to be a great admirer of this very special man: a genius who taught himself to get along with the rest of us who were so distant from his brilliance.

There are only two people that I have willingly called "rabbi." One is Rabbi Steinsaltz and the other was Rabbi Poupko. Even though he gave me permission to call him Yaakov Moshe—and from that point on started introducing himself as Yaakov Moshe—I always called him Rabbi Poupko because of my great respect for him.

S holom loved finding connections between Hebrew words that transferred into English. He'd mention them at every opportunity in his lessons. Here are some that I remember:

Parsha ➤ portion (of the Torah)

Ragil ➤ regular

Beheayma (an animal) ➤ behemoth

Gal aynei ➤ glory, the meaning in Hebrew is "waves of my eyes"

Sholom would give a whole lesson about this saying how God's glory in this world is when we reveal His inner essence. He would say, "Everyone knows the phrase that 'The eyes are the windows the soul'. You see, waves of God's eyes is us revealing His essence."

E very now and then a beggar would come to the door while Sholom was giving his class. Sholom would give me five shekels and ask me to "take care of this."

Once a beggar found the front door open and came in. He interrupted the lesson and asked everyone in the class for *tzedakah*. Sholom was not happy. He told him in Yiddish, "You're disturbing the lesson. I'm giving a lesson now."

The beggar acknowledged Sholom but then ignored him and kept going from person to person asking for money. Sholom looked at me and said, "Barak, take care of this."

I gently helped the beggar find the front door and explained to him that "the Ruv [Rabbi with a Yiddish accent] does not like to be disturbed when teaching." The beggar understood, apologized for the interruption and left.

O ften on Thursday mornings I'd say good morning to Sholom in Batey Rand. He'd ask me how the Wednesday night class went.

Sholom: "Did I say utter nonsense? I actually prepared for this class."

He always asked if he said "utter nonsense." The Brodt's have a book in their bathroom titled *Udder Nonsense*. I immediately thought of the book. I knew that Sholom could give endless classes without preparing anything. Oftentimes he would tell the class to open the Chumash to a certain page, read one line from the Torah and then talk for an entire hour about that line.

Sometimes people would come to the class late and ask me where we were in the Chumash. I'd show them the first line of the *parsha*. "We're still on the first line?" they'd ask.

Photo credit: David Zimand

You
Didn't Need
to Be There

127

A Shtikel Sholom

The third meal at the Brodt's house became Sholom's signature event. It meant so much to him because he knew he was helping people, but also because he finally had the opportunity to express himself fully in speech, song and action.

At some point Sholom decided that he was going to make a disc with the order of the songs that were sung at the third meal at the Brodt's house. Sholom was very excited about this project and told me about each stage as it developed. He often told me how he wanted me to sing with the group that was going to record the disc.

I was happy to participate, but Sholom never told me the recording date. One *Shabbos* I came over for learning in the morning and saw a pile of the third meal discs on a table in the house.

I was a bit crushed. I had really wanted to participate in recording the disc, but I knew better than to say anything. Sholom was a tough teacher at times. I already knew how the whole conversation between us would go.

Instead of complaining to him and asking him why he didn't remember me, I simply wished him a "*mazal tov*" on finishing the discs. He never mentioned it again.

Years later I asked him why he didn't tell me about the recording.

"You didn't need to be there," Sholom said, "and other people did."

That was the end of the conversation.

O nce Rabbi Poupko praised Rabbi Gestetner for putting *tefillin* on people while on a plane ride they shared together from New York to Tel Aviv. I realized after that how important it was and made a decision that I would do the same on my next trip to the States.

I asked Rabbi Gestetner if he had any advice. He suggested that I buy an extra *kippah* because most of the people who will be putting on *tefillin* won't have one.

The plane took off at night. I promised myself in the morning after I davened I would go through the aisles asking Jewish men to put on *tefillin*.

But we arrived so early there was no time. I promised myself on the way back to Israel I would do it, but I lost my nerve. Instead I stood in front of the section of the plane I was in and made sure everyone could clearly see me davening. Afterwards, walking back to my seat, people kept asking me questions about *davening* and *tefillin*. I asked a few people if they were interested in putting on *tefillin* and I was somewhat relieved when they declined.

I told all of this to Sholom after I came back from my trip. I wanted to know what he thought. Did he put *tefillin* on people on his flights?

Sholom: "Once I sit down in the seat, I fall asleep for the entire flight."

He paused for a few seconds, thinking.

"It's an important thing, though. I should really make an effort to put *tefillin* on people on my next trip."

After Sholom's next trip I asked him how it went.

Sholom: "I couldn't help myself. I slept the whole flight. I guess it's not my *shlichut* [mission]. But I have to work on that. Remind me for my next trip."

I came to Sholom a few weeks after Shavuot and told him I was feeling down. Did he have some advice for me.

Sholom: "Of course you're feeling down. First you were preparing for Chanukah, then Purim, then Pesach, then Shavuot and now all of the holidays are over until Rosh Hashana."

Me: "So what do you suggest I do?"

Sholom: "It's time to start preparing for Rosh Hashana."

Me: "Now? Six months before?"

Sholom: "Why not? It will give you something to look forward to you and won't feel down. You'll also have an awesome Rosh Hashana."

130

S holom taught that "the Rebbe was against people using the phrase *kiruv rechokim*, bringing close those that are far away from Judaism.

"The Rebbe said there is no such thing as a Jew who is far away from Judaism. Every Jew is close.

"But *kiruv* to Torah and *mitzvot* is something else. Every Jew has a *neshama* [soul] and the nourishment of the soul comes from Torah and *mitzvot*.

"So, for example, a poor man shows up and says 'I'm hungry,' we don't give them a lecture about bread and what they should eat. We give them a piece of bread.

"You meet a *Yid* [Jew] whose soul is hungry, give them a *mitzvah* to do. Put on *tefillin* with them, give them a coin to put in a *tzedakah* box, give them candles for *Shabbos*; give them a *mitzvah* to do.

"And do this without being judgmental of them in the slightest way possible. You don't know. It could be that this person is eating pepperoni pizza on Yom Kippur, but this person did one *mitzvah* that outweighed all of the *mitzvot* that you did for the last thirty years.

"We're not capable of making these judgements. The *avoda* [work] is to reach a place of true love for our fellow Jews."

Occasionally Sholom would talk about gurus. He told me how he and Reb Shlomo once went into an ashram in Montreal. Shlomo gave a concert there and afterwards many people came over to tell him that they were Jews.

Sholom said, "There are good gurus and evil ones. The good ones will teach you and when they feel that you are ready, will let you go, saying, 'You're a Jew. Now go embrace your Judaism.' But the evil ones will hold on and not let a person go."

Whenever there was a Chabad festival (for example when the first Chabad rebbe was released from prison) and then a *farbrengen*, Sholom wanted to know which *farbrengen* I was going to. He didn't ask in order to go with me, although sometimes he did. He asked to make sure that I was going. There was a period where I told Sholom I was too tired to leave the house at 10 pm and come home at midnight or later (the *farbrengens* often go into the wee hours of the morning).

Sholom would tell me, "Pick a *farbrengen* and go. You have to go. You're a Chabadnik. Every Chabadnik has to go *farbreng*."

At some point, many years ago, I started going to a *farbrengen* on every Chabad holiday. In the morning Sholom would ask me where I went.

Me: "I went to Mayanot."

Sholom: "When did you leave?"

Me: "I left at eleven. I was too tired to stay longer."

Sholom: "I got there at 1 am. That's when things really got started."

A close friend of mine one day revealed to me that he was a Jew for Jesus (a Jewish convert to Christianity who believes he can combine being a Jew and a Christian). I asked Sholom for advice.

He told me to first have a conversation with my friend and see if I could convince him that he should remain a Jew. After that didn't work, I asked Sholom what I should do next.

Sholom: "Engage him in a debate. Argue with him on each point and try to convince him to remain a Jew."

Me: "But I don't know how to do that. Aren't there people who are professionals and know how to do this kind of thing?"

Sholom: "Yes, but they're not his friend. You are. This is your task. Buy some books, watch some videos online and then start with an email to your friend. I'll help you. We'll do this together.

"At the same time try to keep him involved in the community. Invite him for *Shabbos* meals, give him an *aliyah* to the Torah, make him feel important and loved."

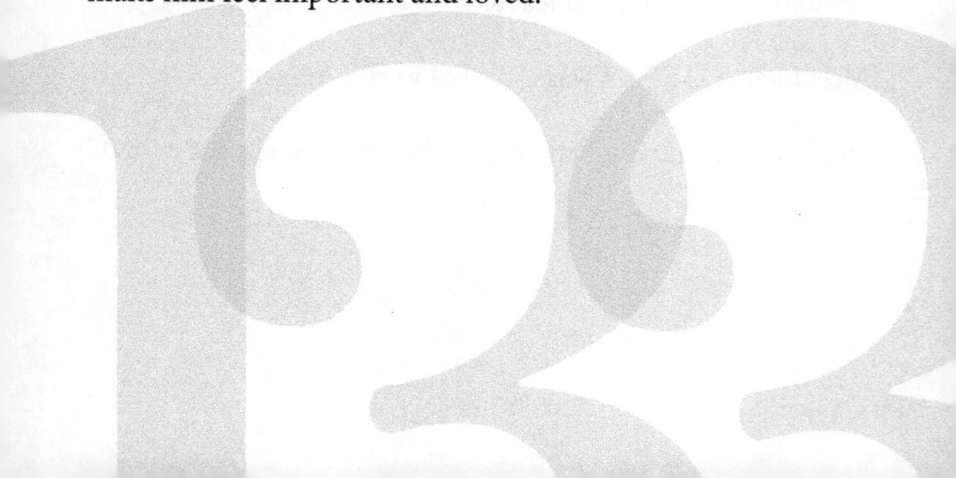

I followed Sholom's instructions and started educating myself in how to argue with a Jew for Jesus. Then I started with an initial email to my friend asking him if he would be willing to engage in an email discussion about being a Jew and believing that Jesus is the Messiah. He agreed and for several months we went back and forth with Sholom reading each email and assisting me in writing the responses.

At some point my friend agreed that my points were valid and that he did not have a good answer, but that it didn't matter, he had "let Jesus into [his] heart" and that's all that mattered. Our correspondence went on for six months. I invited him to our house for meals and made sure he felt welcomed in our *shul*. But nothing could sway my friend from his decision to become a Christian.

"Now what?" I asked Sholom.

Sholom: "We've done all we could to help him. Now you have to cut him off completely."

Me: "Completely?"

Sholom: "You can't help him. At this point he's a heretic and must be cut off from the community. You are not allowed to interact with him any more."

I started ignoring my friend. It wasn't easy. This happened many years ago. I still see this friend occasionally and now allow myself to say "Shalom" to him but nothing more.

A family in our community was broken up by a divorce. The father moved to another country and left several young children behind in Jerusalem. Sholom was very close to this family. I also knew them, but not as well as Sholom.

After the youngest boy in the family became *bar mitzvah* Sholom told me to start looking after him.

Me: "What do you mean 'to look after him'? In what way?"

Sholom: "His father is gone and he needs a father now. You and I are going to be his father. You see him in *shul* in the mornings, right?"

Me: "Yes."

Sholom: "Good, every time you see him just ask him how he's doing. Have a conversation with him and try to give him some advice. You're good at that. You talk with people all the time."

The next time I saw the boy I engaged him in a conversation. Sholom was right. This boy was lost and needed a father figure. Every now and then Sholom would ask if I was talking with the boy and he'd tell me how he was helping him. We did this together for many years until the boy was drafted into the army. I still see him around occasionally and keep engaging him in short conversations when I can.

S holom was once hosting Reb Shlomo at a third meal on *Shabbos* in Montreal. He said Reb Shlomo was exhausted, looked over at Sholom and closed his eyes to rest. All of a sudden Sholom felt like Shlomo had lent him his singing voice. He said he'd never had a voice like that before or after.

Sholom was singing the melodies during the meal and at some point he started paying attention to this amazing voice Reb Shlomo had lent him. As soon as he did, Shlomo woke up and stared at Sholom with a look that said "you blew it."

"As soon as I started paying attention to my voice," Sholom said, "I lost it, literally. Shlomo woke up and took his voice back."

Then turning to me, Sholom asked, "Barak, when you lead the *davening* on Friday night, do you hear your voice?"

"If I do, I get worried and start to look at the words in the *siddur* or look around the *shul* at the congregation. I try to never get to the point where I hear my own voice."

Sholom: "Ah, that's why the *davening* is so good."

Once Sholom and I were walking to the *mikva* on *Shabbos* morning. We passed by an old *shul* in the neighborhood. "Do you mind if we see if it's open?" Sholom asked.

We walked over to the *shul*. No one was there, but the door was open. We went inside. Right away I could feel the *kedusha* (holiness) of the *shul*. I asked Sholom if he also felt it. Even though he knew there was such a thing as being sensitive to holiness, he said he didn't feel anything.

I told him about the first time I opened the *Aron Kodesh* (holy ark) in Batey Rand. "It was like a gust of wind coming out of the Aron. I felt like a fan of kedusha was blowing on me."

Sholom told me about some people who could feel holiness in physical objects. "You could put two books in a person's hands and they could tell you which one was *kodesh* [holy] or not."

When we got back to his house to learn, Sholom wanted to try it. He told me to give him a dictionary and a holy book with his eyes closed. Then he did it for me. Neither of us got it right.

In the early days of the Mayanot *shul* when hardly anyone showed up in the mornings, I was there with Sholom. I didn't know him so well back then. Sholom had led *Shacharit* (the morning service) and took the Torah out of the ark at the end. He brought it through the men's section and then without thinking twice walked with the Torah scroll straight through the women's section. I'd never seen this done in an Orthodox *shul*. Even if he wasn't leading the *davening*, he'd take the Torah scroll from whoever was holding it and carry it from the back of the women's section to the front and then back into the men's section every time.

S holom was once at a wedding in Great Neck, New York. It was one of these country club type places with two wedding halls.

Sholom arrived a little early. He was waiting for the elevator and this guy comes in dressed in jeans and a leather jacket. Sholom could see he had just parked his motorcycle outside.

Next to the elevator was a little area where you could leave a coat or photography equipment; an area for the service staff. Sholom saw this guy going into the service area. He didn't know who he was. But he heard him talking and it turned out that he was the rabbi for the wedding in the other hall.

"The language he was using, I'm telling you, I know a lot of words, there were words that I didn't even know. I'm thinking to myself, man, what kind of *chupah* [wedding] is he going to put on?"

This guy put on a white silk robe, a *kippah* and a *tallit*, "and now he looks like a 'real rabbi,' you know."

An hour later Sholom had to go outside to the rental car and get something. When he took the elevator down he saw this guy already back in the service area taking off his robe and gathering his things, wearing again his leather jacket and jeans. He'd finished his job already.

"And thank God, as I saw this guy, I remembered Reb Nachman's teaching of seeing the good points in a person and focusing on the good in them. So, I focused on something positive in him and immediately, he turns around and says to me, '*Sholom aleichem*.'"

I asked Sholom, "Do you remember what the positive thing was?"

"No, and it doesn't matter."

"We get into the elevator together and he asks me in English, 'So, where are you from?' I tell him I'm from *Yerushalim* [Jerusalem].

"Then he asks me, 'Where do you think I'm from?'

"I tell him 'I have no idea. Where are you from?'

"He says, 'I'm from Mea Shearim, from the Reb Arelach *chassidim* [one of the hard core *charedi chassidic* groups that wear the gold and blue striped robes]. My whole family lives in Mea Shearim, my brothers, sisters, parents, everyone is there.

"He said thirty years ago he came to America to be an assistant rabbi, *chazan*, whatever, and he says, 'Look at me now. I thought I was going to do something good for *Yiddishkeit* [Judaism].' And with tears in his eyes he says to me, 'And look at me now. And my children? Don't even ask me about my kids.'

Sholom concluded, "Just like you have to see the good in people, you also have a see the good in the Land of Israel. In order to see the good in the Land of Israel, you have to be very, very humble."

Every year at *Seudat Moshiach* (the *Chassidic* gathering during the last hours of Passover) I tell a *Chassidic* story. Once I told Rebbe Nachman's story of *The Rabbi's Only Son*. The story is about a great Torah scholar (the son) who was looking for a great teacher to guide him. At the end of the story, Rebbe Nachman says that the rabbi's son was the "little light" and the teacher the "great light." Had the two of them come together Moshiach would have come.

Afterwards Sholom came over to me, "So you're the little light?"

Me: "I'm certainly not a Torah scholar, but I am looking for you to guide me. Does that mean you're the 'great light'?"

Sholom just smiled.

S holom and I disagreed on the meaning of a Torah concept during one of the lessons.

I answered him with the classic joke, "Two Jews, three opinions."

Sholom: "That's all?"

141

This is one of my favorite Sholom stories. A couple of Kotzk *chassidim* met a *misnaged* (someone opposed to the *chassidim*) during their journey to see the Kotzker Rebbe.

The *chassidim* try to convince the *misnaged* to come with them to their rebbe.

"I'm not interested in rebbes. I don't believe in this whole *chassidus* nonsense."

The *chassidim* insisted.

"Give me one good reason why I should come to your rebbe. Just one. Go ahead," said the *misnaged*.

One of the *chassidim* answered, "You know, our rebbe is endowed with special powers and as his *chassidim* we also have received some of those special powers."

"Oh yeah? Like what?" said the skeptical *misnaged*.

"Like reading minds."

"What? You're telling me you can read my mind?"

"Yes. Absolutely. I know what you're thinking right now."

"Oh yeah! What am thinking about right now? Go ahead. Tell me."

"That's an easy one. You're thinking about *Hashem*."

"Ha!" laughed the *misnaged*. "No I'm not."

"You're not thinking about *Hashem*? Quick! You need to come with us to our rebbe. He'll fix that."

S ometimes there would be so many people squeezed into the Brodt's house that Sholom would tell this story.

"I remember being in the Witt's house when Shlomo would teach. People just kept coming in. It got to the point where you really had to squeeze your way into the house. Reb Shlomo told us, '*Chevre* [friends], please make yourselves small.'

"When even more people kept squeezing in, Reb Shlomo said, 'Holy brothers and sisters, please, I'm begging you, we have to love each other more.' "

Every time I have to squeeze into the *mikva* or on a bus, I turn to the person next to me and say, "We just have to love each other more." They always look at me like I'm a little crazy.

143

Akiva Goldberg reminded me of this story that Sholom would often tell.

Two friends grew up together in the same town and one moved away. Many years later the friend that left came home for a visit. When he arrived there was a crowd gathered in the town square anxiously waiting for someone to be hanged. As the out of town friend came closer he realized that it was his old friend who was about to be hanged.

He asked in the crowd what happened. Upon hearing the story, he realized that his friend was innocent and ran onto the platform and told the hangman that he, himself was guilty. The hangman didn't care who would hang for the crime and so he took the out of town friend and put the noose on his neck. When the friend who was just released realized that it was his old friend who took his place he insisted that he really was the guilty one and to hang him instead. This went for some time, until it was decided to send them both to the king to decide who would be hanged.

The king met the two friends and asked them what was going on. They explained to him that they were friends from youth and when the out of town friend saw his old friend about to be hanged he knew he was innocent. He couldn't bear to see his friend be hanged and insisted he be hanged instead. When the other friend saw his out of town friend about to be hanged he couldn't bear to see it and asked to be hanged instead.

The king said he would let them both go, clear that they were innocent. But on one condition, "The two of you need to let me be your friend."

S holom told a story about a woman who was one of the founding parents of a religious school in America. She helped found the school so her children could get a Jewish education since there were no other religious schools anywhere nearby. After a couple of years the principal quit and the school fell apart. This woman decided that for her own children's education she would take over the school and get it back into shape. She put her heart and soul into helping—without getting paid for her work—and brought it back to being a thriving school with even more students enrolled than before. The next year the school hired a new principal, thanking this woman for all she'd done.

She was livid and could not release her anger. She came to Sholom for help, telling him that she would have happily taken the position as principal but no one even offered her the job.

Sholom told her, "Imagine your children will face a similar problem in the future and because of what you've been through you will be able to advise them and help them get through it. If you knew that's why *Hashem* put you through this, would it help?"

I asked Sholom what made him think of this advice. He told me a story about a man who had come to the Lubavitcher Rebbe. His son had died and he was inconsolable. He simply could not function. But after being in the Rebbe's room he came out smiling, a completely changed man.

The Rebbe's secretary asked him what the Rebbe had said. "He told me to imagine my son was still alive, but on the other side of the world. I could not visit him or receive letters back from him, but I could send him letters and gifts from where I live. If I knew one hundred percent for sure that my son would receive all of my letters and gifts, would that be a comfort for me?

"When I told the Rebbe 'yes' he told me that's exactly the situation. 'Your son can hear you when you *daven* for his soul and his soul will benefit from all of the *mitzvot* you do for him in this world. And eventually when your souls will be united you will see that I was right.' "

After writing an entire book about Sholom the second to last piece is Sholom writing about me.

Sholom always asked how my first book was coming along. A month before he died, Sholom wrote me this poem the day after I showed him the cover of my first book, *Figure It Out When You Get There.*

You'll figure it out when you get there
journeys
going arriving staying leaving
moving forward backward
sideways up down up
higher
circles spirals confusion clarity
fear love awe
sure unsure
trusting sincere confident
honest just generous
grateful love friendship
love jealous egoist
dark lost disconnected
falling standing jumping dancing
alive open vulnerable
it all doesn't make sense
but you'll figure it out when you get there
in the meantime sing dance
learn celebrate b'simcha (with joy)
(for Barak, may his light shine)

He originally wrote "you'll know when you get there" and asked me, "That's the title right?"

When I told him it wasn't, but it didn't matter, Sholom told me "when you read it just change the words to figure it out when you get there."

Of all the short little notes and dedications Sholom wrote to me over our years together in this world, this one means the most.

S holom would always say "Shalom" to people on the street. When I asked him why, he said, "Shalom is *Hashem's* name. So when you say 'Shalom' to someone, you're bringing God into their lives."

After that I started saying "Shalom" to people on the street as well. Any time a person looked at me, I'd say "Shalom."

I got into the habit and once said "Shalom" to someone in the bathroom in my office building. He got angry at me and said, "You don't say that word in the bathroom! But thank you for saying 'hi' to me."

Then I saw on *Shabbos* Sholom would say "Shabbat Shalom" or "*Gut Shabbos*" to everyone we passed on the street; even people on their cell phones or driving their cars.

When I asked him why, he said that when people say "Shabbat Shalom" or "*Gut Shabbos*" back, they're acknowledging that it's *Shabbos*. Even if they just nod, that's also an acknowledgment. And since the reward for a *mitzvah* is a *mitzvah*, that is, one *mitzvah* leads to another, "God willing, eventually they will want more of *Shabbos*."

After that I started saying *Gut Shabbos* to everyone I passed on the street, also to people on their cell phones or driving.

Sholom warned me, however, "You have to make sure to say it with true love and not as criticism. Do you think anyone will want to keep *Shabbos* after rocks were thrown at them?!" In some Haredi neighborhoods people throw rocks at cars that pass by and shout at them "*Shabbos! Shabbos!*"

I sat with Sholom's body the *Shabbos* before his burial. On the walk back I thought I was taking a shortcut by going past the Israel Museum. It turns out that it was the longer way, but I only realized that half way through when it was taking much longer than I thought it should to get to *shul*.

Along the way I saw many people exercising. Some were running, others were walking. Some had on headphones and ignored me, others said "Shabbat Shalom" back to me.

I had the opportunity to say "Shabbat Shalom" to many Jews that might not have had a chance to connect with *Shabbos* otherwise. Since Sholom taught me how to say it, I made sure to say Shabbat Shalom from a place of true love for my fellow Jews. As I saw them running towards me, I'd say in my head "Love your fellow Jew unconditionally" and then say "Shabbat Shalom."

I read a quote in the book *Tuesdays With Morrie*, "Death is the end of the body but not the end of the relationship." Even though Sholom had passed away, his teaching continues.

Epilogue

I wrote these stories over a period of six months from the day that Sholom passed away. The stories give you a small glimpse into who Sholom was and my relationship with him. That's why my wife, Noga, suggested we call the book *A Shtikel Sholom*, meaning a little bit of Sholom. It was also the blessing that Netzach gave us all at his father's funeral. That we all be a little bit of Sholom.

Shlomo Katz and I spoke shortly after Sholom died. He was having a hard time accepting the void that Sholom left behind. I told Shlomo, "We just got a promotion. Whatever you were doing to help the Jewish people before, just became more important."

That's how I see my role as well. When a great person passes away, those who were close to that person need to pick up some small piece of the work they were doing and make it their own, just like Moshe *Rabeinu* after Aharon and Miriam passed away.

The morning after we buried Sholom I told my wife, Noga, about this funny short conversation we had a few *Shabboses* before he died. Noga told me to post it on Facebook. Here's the first post again:

Sholom and I were learning on *Shabbos* morning. He paused with his finger still on the place where we were learning.

Sholom: "Barak, why are you so fat?"

Me: "Sholom, why do you look like you're 90 years old?"

He went back to the learning as if we'd never stopped.

That was our relationship: honest, loving, serious and humorous. I made Sholom my rabbi, my teacher and my mentor. He didn't ask for it. Not only did he not ask for it, he flat out refused. He constantly pushed me away. In part it was his personality and in part he didn't want "to be anyone's rabbi," in his words. But I wouldn't give up. No matter how many times he pushed me away, I would come back for more.

I knew Sholom was something special from the first day I started learning with him. I had met the Lubavitcher Rebbe once but was too scared to see him again; it was such an intense experience. I never met Reb Shlomo.

I realized that Sholom was it for me. He was my connection to Reb Shlomo and my connection to all of the great *Chassidim* and Chassidic rebbes, rabbis and rebbetzins that I never met or even knew existed. I made sure to make the most of every second I spent with him. I was consistently conscious.

After the first post Chaya Kaplan-Lester asked for 30 posts for the first 30 days following Sholom's burial. I had no idea how I could come up with 30 posts, but then the ideas kept coming.

Every week I would sit for an hour or so and write that week's posts. It was a huge comfort for me. I needed it as I know many people who knew Sholom did too.

We shared this time together, remembering our friend and our teacher. Some people have written telling me that they never met Sholom, but my stories helped them to learn from him. Others who didn't know him so well got to know him better and those of us who knew him well enjoyed reliving special moments with him.

My wife Noga once posed a theoretical question. "Where would we live if Jews couldn't live in *Eretz Yisrael*: New York, or California?"

I knew exactly where we would live, "Wherever Sholom is that's where we'll be."

Noga: "What, even if he moved to Iceland?"

Me: "It really doesn't matter as long as Sholom is there."

P.S. Sweetest friends the stories are not over! The whole reason I started writing these stories is because I have written an entire book of stories like these about my life and the people who inspired me. If you enjoyed reading my stories, you'll love my book. You can learn more about it at barakhullman.com.

Also, I encourage you to buy Sholom's book, *Exodus: The Model of Personal Liberation*, available on Amazon. You can find hundreds of Sholom's lessons on YouTube by searching for the Simchat Shlomo channel.

Acknowledgements

Several people helped improve the quality of this book. I want to thank Nechama Wells, Sharon Saunders, Ali Smith, Ourit Ben Haim, Folli Tessler, Faige Chaye Meor, Linda Brownstein and Vera Schwarcz for their time, skills and talents.

Thank you to my wife, Noga, for the initial idea to post my first story about Sholom on Facebook and for suggesting the title of the book. Also for being such a supportive and loving wife.

I tried to find out who took the images of Sholom included in the book. If an image does not have a credit it was because no one claimed credit for it.

This whole book is a way to say thank you to Sholom who changed my life for the better. May his memory be for a blessing.

And thank you to *Hashem* for making me a Jew.

Glossary

Aliyah,
    to go up.

Baal Teshuva,
    (a returnee to a religious
    Jewish life)

Baruch Hashem,
    "blessed is God," thank
    God.

Bentching,
    praying.

Bima,
    raised section where the
    Torah is read.

Birkat hamazon,
    blessing after eating bread.

Bracha,
    blessing.

Chas v'shalom,
    God forbid.

Chassid,
    follower of a Rebbe

Chassidim,
    plural of chassid.

Chazzan,
    cantor.

Cheder,
    religious school.

Chevra kadisha,
    burial society

Chevruta,
    learning partner

Chevre,
    friends.

Daven,
    to pray.

Davening,
    prayers.

D'var Torah,
    word of Torah.

Eretz Yisrael,
    the land of Israel

Eruv,
    a rabbinical extension of a
    person's home so that Jews
    can carry objects on the
    Sabbath.

Etrog,
    citrus fruit used on Sukkot

Galach,
    priest.

Hashem,
    "the Name," meaning God.

Kaddish,
    prayer for the deceased.

Kashrut,
kosher.

Kiddish,
blessing on wine.

Kippah,
see Yarmulke.

Kodesh,
holy.

L'chaim,
"to life".

Mikva,
ritual pool.

Mincha,
afternoon prayer.

Mitzvah,
commandment from God.

Minyan,
prayer quorum of ten
Jewish men.

Misnaged,
Misnagdim, those that
opposed the Chassidim.

Mitzvot,
commandments from God.

Motzei Shabbos,
after the Sabbath has ended

Neshamah, soul.

Niggun,
Chassidic tune.

Peyos,
religious sidelocks.

Parnasah,
livelihood.

Parsha,
Torah portion.

Rebbe,
Chassidic master.

Refuah shelaimah,
full recovery.

Seder,
order.

Shabbos or Shabbat,
the Jewish *Sabbath*, from
Friday night sunset to
Saturday night sunset.

Shalom aleichem,
peace unto you. The
standard greeting between
two religious Jews.

Sheitel,
wig worn by religious
Jewish women to keep their
hair from being exposed.

Shofar,
> a ram's horn used as a musical instrument mainly on Rosh Hashanah (the Jewish New Year). It is a holy object used also for prayer.

Shuk,
> an open air marketplace for produce.

Shul,
> synagogue.

Shulchan Aruch,
> book of Jewish law.

Shtender,
> the podium at the front of a shul, also a book stand.

Shtreimel,
> fur hat.

Siddur,
> prayer book.

Simchat Torah,
> holiday celebrating the completion of one cycle of reading the Torah.

Tallis or tallit,
> prayer shawl.

Teshuva,
> come back to God

Tefillin,
> leather boxes containing scrolls of parchment inscribed with verses from the Torah.

Tzadik,
> totally righteous person.

Tzedakah,
> charity.

Tzitziot or tzitzis,
> strings and knots worn by Jewish men on four cornered garments. Even though most people don't wear four cornered garments, religious Jewish men wear a special garment so they can put tzitziot on it and fulfill the commandment.

Yarmulke or kippah,
> Jewish head cover for men.

Yahrzeit,
> the anniversary of some-one's death

Yetzer Ha'ra,
> evil inclination.

About
Sholom Brodt

Sholom Brodt studied in yeshivot in Montreal, Toronto and Jerusalem and held an M.A. degree in Jewish Education from the Yeshiva University in New York. Sholom received his rabbinic ordination from Reb Shlomo Carlebach in 1989. Inspired by Reb Shlomo's vibrant style of Torah, Sholom and his wife, Judy, founded Yeshivat Simchat Shlomo in 2001. Before his passing in 2017 he taught daily and weekly *Chassidut* classes at the yeshiva, which is located in Nachlaot, Jerusalem. In the footsteps of Reb Shlomo, Sholom traveled several times a year, visiting, reaching out and teaching in diverse communities across North America and Europe.

The author and Sholom during a Wednesday night parsha lesson.

About
the Author

Photo by Roni Isaiah

B arak Hullman is a storyteller, writer, entrepreneur and marketer. He moved to Jerusalem, Israel in 1995 to study for a PhD in Islamic studies where he met his wife, Noga. They have seven children. When Barak is not writing he's usually cooking, throwing pottery, singing, telling stories or planning his next project.

Website: barakhullman.com
Facebook: fb.me/barakauthor
Twitter: @barakhullman

Wait,
There's More!

If you enjoyed this book, you'll love my first book *Figure It Out When You Get There: A Memoir of Stories About Living Life First and Watching How Everything Falls In Line* which is available on Amazon.com and also from the author at barakhullman.com.

I've included the first three chapters in the pages below.

FIGURE IT OUT
WHEN YOU
GET THERE

A Memoir of Stories About Living Life First and
Watching How Everything Else Falls In Line

BARAK HULLMAN

MUFFIN TOPS

I first started writing this book as a philosophy of life using personal stories to help explain the ideas. When I showed my wife the first chapter she told me, "Honestly, the stories are much more interesting. Why don't you just write a book of personal stories?"

It reminded me of a Seinfeld episode where one of the characters opens a bakery that just sells the tops of muffins, since that's the part that everyone likes best.

This is a book of muffin tops.

Plant and water a watermelon seed and under the right circumstances you'll get a watermelon. Each watermelon will taste and look different. Plant and water me and you'll get a very Jewish book.

There's a glossary of Hebrew/Yiddish terms in the back.

SOMETIMES I'VE WANTED TO THANK THAT IDIOTIC KID

The Boy Scouts saved my life. I was such a poor student in school that, without the validation I got from the Boy Scouts, I don't know where I would have ended up. I didn't have the mental energy to "apply myself" as the adults in my life liked to say. But the Boy Scouts was full of adventure, challenges, respect, honor, freedom, independence, and a chance to use all of my God-given talents. Within a few months of joining, I was made a patrol leader. I barely understood how the Scouts worked when I started leading a group of ten boys at thirteen years old, but it was what I needed. It was like a really strong cup of coffee when you've been sleeping for so long you can't seem to wake up.

I flew through the ranks and quickly became the "Senior Patrol Leader." This meant I was effectively running the entire troop of thirty-plus boys. I was fifteen years old; the youngest Senior Patrol Leader in the troop's history. The boys looked up to me. They phoned me at home. They confided in me. They asked me questions about how to deal with their parents' divorce or the bully in school. I went from a bored kid with no direction to a young man with purpose and a fire in his heart. I'm still that young man, just physically older and with a bigger fire than back then. I thank God every day for the Boy Scouts.

The Order of the Arrow is like the Honor Society of the Boy Scouts. You can only be admitted by troop nomination. Then you need to do additional volunteer work in your community. Afterwards, you go through what we called "The Ordeal." It lasted for two days. You fasted during the day, as you worked fixing roofs in the local national park and slept in the woods with no tent or sleeping bag. There was no talking during the daytime and we had a big feast at the end of the work day.

A year after being admitted to the Order of the Arrow, I became one of the leaders in my chapter. This ratcheted-up the community volunteering. The usual was fixing rundown buildings in public institutions or volunteering in a soup kitchen or a homeless shelter. A good friend of mine at the time had a dream to start a Boy Scout troop in the poorest, most violent part of downtown Miami; Overtown it was called. Would I help?

"No way!" was my first answer. "I'm not going to get myself killed over a Boy Scout troop." He told me that starting the troop would be enough to get the leadership position that I wanted in the Order of the Arrow (he was the head of the committee that decided on the leadership positions; if he recommended me, I was in) and that we would do it in the Baptist Church, which was a safe haven in the neighborhood. He'd already done the groundwork. Everything was ready. He just needed someone motivated like me to start the troop. He promised to drive me there himself and, if anything ever happened, I was free to never return again.

I agreed and the next week we drove into Overtown in my friend's car, an old Mustang without seatbelts. I joked with him that I wasn't sure what was more dangerous: driving in his car or going into Overtown. I grew up in South Florida. I had driven past Overtown a hundred times on my way to work at my father's eyeglass store on Miami Beach but I never got off on the Overtown exit until now. The sun had set as we were driving down South. We turned off in darkness, right into the worst neighborhood in Miami.

Overtown spelled riots, shootings, open drug use and prostitutes selling their wares. I had mentally prepared myself for what I might see, but it was worse than I had imagined. We stopped at the first light and several people came over to us. Of course, we didn't open the window, but one tried to sell us drugs and another was a prostitute.

The traffic lights changed and we kept driving until we reached the Baptist Church; a modest building with a white picket fence and a trim lawn.

From the parking lot, we walked into the church without a problem. The church choir was practicing in the main church and we were in a back room. The boys were waiting for us; I was in charge. My friend said if I needed anything he'd be in the church office. I introduced myself and started working my Boy Scout magic. Within a few months the boys were really shaping up. I was elected to the leadership position I was working toward.

The Order of the Arrow was based on Native American traditions. We wore full Native American clothes with headdresses, shoes, warpaint; the works. The headdresses were provided for us; the rest we had to buy or make ourselves. Only a few of the "brothers" were allowed to wear these costumes. There were ceremonies related to the Order of the Arrow and a book with entire speeches to memorize for each ceremony.

As a leader of the chapter, I played the part of an ancient Native American elder during the induction ceremony for new brothers into the Order of the Arrow. It was a beautiful ceremony. The costume was authentic and impressive.

We were in the heart of the forest. Leading up to the area where I began my speech was a path lit up with little fires in tin cans. Each had a roll of toilet paper soaked in some type of flammable liquid. Behind me was a large bonfire that I had lit.

I was given a five gallon plastic jug of gasoline and a cup to top up the tin cans. I was told "always use the cup." Got it. Always use the cup. I had a few groups of inductees come and go to my station already. I checked the book to make sure I wasn't forgetting any lines from my speech. Then I fed the bonfire and walked with the jug of gasoline to check the tin can fires. Some of them were running low. I poured the gas into the cup and then into the tin can. But this seemed so inefficient. Why bother with the cup when I could just pour the gasoline directly from the jug? I quickly learned why.

As I was pouring the gasoline from the five gallon jug, the fire jumped from the tin can up the stream of gasoline and the jug exploded. The gas was all over my body and I was on fire. There was no one around. We had picked this remote location so that no one could even see the bonfire. The new inductees were brought blindfolded until they reached the fire-lit path.

When I was a kid, I spent a lot of time watching TV. There were commercials from Smokey the Bear in which he would say, "Only you can prevent forest fires." Oy vey, Smokey. I really blew that one. Then I remembered this commercial I'd seen over and over. If you catch on fire, "Stop, drop and roll." At last, TV had done me some good. Within a split second of catching on fire, I stopped, dropped and rolled and, it turns out, it works! I had a sunburn, but nothing more. I quickly took off my burned clothes and stamped on them. Fortunately I still had on my shorts and a t-shirt that I'd been wearing under the Native American costume. I was fine, thank God, but now I had another problem; a raging forest fire that I had started and no one there to help me put it out.

We were in a Boy Scout camp, a tract of forest bought by the Boy Scouts a hundred years before. I knew there were other troops camping out there. Realizing the severity of the fire, I ran faster than I had ever run in my life on the dirt roads until I found a troop. I ran into their campground and explained as quickly as possible to the Scoutmaster what had happened. He couldn't believe it. I showed him the fire in the distance. Then he sprung into action. He called the whole troop together, maybe forty boys, and told them, "We're going to put out that forest fire."

We ran back to where the fire was. My spot was above a lake with a beautiful view. We grabbed buckets and made an assembly line from the lake to the fire. I was the deepest in the lake filling up the buckets with water. We would send bucket after bucket up the hill to the fire. In the meantime the fire department had been called, but they were about fifteen minutes away. My biceps were spent pulling up buckets of water from the lake. My arms were quivering from exhaustion, but only death would have stopped me sending water up the line.

Eventually the fire was put out. It was a massive fire. This was summertime in Miami, in a tinder-dry forest, acres of which were consumed. The camp ranger asked me what happened. I told him the truth and he freaked out, "Didn't anyone tell you to use the cup?"

Ten years or so later, I went back to the forest. I went on my own, not with any Scout troop or for any organized event. I tried to find the part that I had burned down, but I couldn't. There was a new camp ranger at the time. I went to his house and told him I was there the night the huge forest fire happened and could he please tell me where the burned part of the forest was. He looked at me like a police detective.

It seemed like he was about to say to me, "Are you the kid that burned it down?" but he didn't. He said the burned part of the forest had grown back already and, "Whoever burned it down actually did us a big favor." It had been an old part of the forest and many of the trees were dead. The fire had burned down a lot of the old, dead trees and now it's the most beautiful part of the forest. "Sometimes I've wanted to thank that idiotic kid for what he did," the camp ranger said to me, and then he changed his mind. "No, if I ever met him, I'd tell him what an idiot he was."

KING DAVID'S DIRECT DESCENDANT

A lot of the beggars of Jerusalem know me because I treat them with respect. Some of them know me by name and know a little bit about me. Some know where I live. Some have my phone number. I try to help as many people as I can without endangering myself or my family. The beggars of Jerusalem are pretty harmless anyway.

There was one beggar whose name was David. He was originally from the Southwest of America and had somehow or another ended up in Jerusalem. He lived in a cave in the Jerusalem forest full of water bottles and personal items. David said he was preparing for the end of the world.

He used to play a little drum and sing a tune while collecting money on the street. A lot of the beggars I know just ask for money, but he made an effort. He would sing, "*Daveed melech yisrael chai, chai v'kayam*" (King David of the Jewish people lives, lives forever).

Every time I saw him I gave him a few coins and asked him how he was doing. He always had the same answer, "I'm gonna make it. I'm gonna make it." Then he would pull out some papers with thoughts he wrote down. They made no sense to me at all. He was obsessed with showing his direct lineage to King David. Sometimes he thought he was King David reincarnated.

I thought to myself, sure, he's crazy and lives in a cave, of course he thinks he's gonna "make it." Make what exactly? Was this called "making it?" Time and again I would come across David on the street and we'd have the same conversation.

I've had a lot of hard times in my adult life and, when I would hear David saying he was going to make it, I would think, if *he's* gonna make it, then for sure *I'm* gonna make it. I even started using his phrase. People would ask me how I'm doing and I'd tell them "I'm gonna make it." This phrase often gave me strength in my hardest of times. I repeated it to myself over and over again "I'm gonna make it. I'm gonna make it."

David was in and out of homeless shelters, kind people's homes, prison and the hospital, and then back on the streets again. Sometimes David was around and other times you wouldn't see him for weeks or even months.

One day I asked a friend of mine who knew David well where he was. "He didn't make it," was his answer.

"What?" I asked. "He died?"

"Yep," my friend said, "he didn't make it."

Or maybe he did. After all, what are we all here for? You have this success or the other, but we all leave this world eventually. We're just leaves, piled on top of older leaves making up the ground for the next generation to walk on.

David left a legacy, at least with me. He didn't have a family or a home, but he had an optimistic message for anyone who was willing to stop and listen to him. Thanks to David, I have found the strength to continue when it seems like all life has given me are dead ends. I just keep repeating to myself, "I'm gonna make it. I'm gonna make it." And eventually I do.

GET ON A PLANE AND NEVER COME BACK HERE AGAIN

One of my closest friends from Jerusalem was getting married in New York at the age of forty-six. It was his first time getting married. I told him years before that when he got married, if I could afford it, I would fly in from Jerusalem for the wedding. My business had done better than usual and, with my wife's permission, I booked flights to visit my family in South Florida and then to go to my friend's wedding in New York. He was getting married on a Sunday. We spent *Shabbos* (the Jewish Sabbath) together in Crown Heights, Brooklyn.

Sunday morning we went to *daven* (pray) at 770 Eastern Parkway, Chabad International Headquarters. It's a *minyan* (prayer quorum) factory there. Every few minutes a new *minyan* was starting. We found a *minyan* to *daven* with. I had quite a few things in my *tallis* bag and, since it was the month of Elul, I also had my shofar (a ram's horn used as a musical instrument). I had packed the shofar at the top of the bag so it wouldn't knock into anything when I was travelling.

This was the shofar that my parents gave me when I was thirteen, at my Bar Mitzvah. I used to blow the shofar in our synagogue for Rosh Hashanah (the Jewish New Year). It was a beautiful shofar with a great sound. I started playing the French Horn when I was thirteen and all of those years of practice made playing the shofar feel like a piece of cake. Over the years I blew the shofar during the Rosh Hashanah services and always got compliments, which led to people wanting to see my shofar. The shofar itself also got compliments.

After I finished *davening* at the *minyan* at 770, I noticed my friend was deep in prayer. It was his wedding day. He'd waited a long time to get married, having friends that were already grandparents at his age. This was a big day for him and he wanted to thank God for it through prayer. I understood that and occupied myself with learning Torah. We left 770 half an hour later.

We had a whole schedule planned for the morning. We quickly packed our things and left. By two o'clock we were at the wedding hall, four hours early. I saw my friend was well taken care of and I went outside for a little walk. I had over three hours left until the wedding began. No one was taking pictures of me.

The wedding was in the heart of the American Chassidic community in Williamsburg. Even though I had lived in New Jersey for several years before moving to Israel, I had never been to Williamsburg. Besides seeing my aging grandparents, visiting Chassidic Williamsburg was the highlight of my trip.

It was a little shocking. I'm used to being around a lot of Jews—I live in Jerusalem, after all—but not in Brooklyn. I'd never seen anything like this, even in Mea Shearim. All of the store signs were in Yiddish. The men were dressed in black, the women with their *sheitels* (wigs) and strollers. I loved all of this Jewish energy. I felt that, after a week in the States and feeling out of place as a Jew, I was finally amongst my people.

But I wasn't. I don't speak Yiddish. I speak Hebrew and English. I know a few phrases in Yiddish, but I'm not Haredi. So, as much as I loved seeing all of these Jews, they didn't seem to love me back so much. I stood out like a red balloon amongst a stadium of black balloons, but I didn't really care.

I walked around like I was in Disneyland. I passed by a row of school buses filled with little Yiddish-speaking kids with their checkered shirts and *peyos* (sidelocks). I was so excited to see these kids that I was crying and laughing at the same time. I can't really explain it. I just felt a deep connection with them.

I blew the kids kisses in the air; me on the street, them on the school buses. The kids stuck out their tongues at me and laughed so hard they fell off of the seats. Then their teacher came over with a big smile and started speaking to me in Hebrew. "You must be from Israel. Are you from Jerusalem?" he asked me. I couldn't believe it.

"How do you know?" I answered him in Hebrew.

He had a big smile on his face and said, "I've seen this before. It's been years since I've seen it, but you must be from Jerusalem if you're acting like this." Then he gave me a big hug and told me he needed to see me blowing kisses in the air to the kids more than I needed to blow the kisses. I kissed him on the cheek and told him I loved him. I was just overwhelmed with a love for the Jewish People; my people.

I kept walking for an hour. I knew it would take an hour to walk back. I went into stores, bought some coffee and pastries, then went into a toy store and bought "Mitzvoh Kinder" (*mitzvah* kids), which were little plastic dolls of kids with *tzitziot* and *kippot*. I bought them for my wife, who studied Yiddish. She had asked me to see if I could find them on my trip. What a surprise to find them so easily. I went into bookstores and just about any store to see the Jews working and buying there. After an hour I started walking back; taking in all of the buildings and the people.

Sometime on *Shabbos* my friend and I were talking about where he was going to stay after the wedding. He told me it was a secret location and he couldn't tell me. His future wife didn't want anyone to know where they would be staying on their wedding night.

I told him, "No problem. I'm staying at the Hyatt Hotel in Midtown." He couldn't believe it.

"No way. That's where we're staying." Now I couldn't believe it. He told me he promised to get his future wife a room in a beautiful Manhattan hotel and picked this one. We joked how funny it would be if we ran into each other in the hotel lobby after the wedding. Then he realized it wouldn't be so funny since it was meant to be a "secret location."

When I arrived at the hotel, I asked the guy helping me with my bags if he'd seen a bride and groom come in before me. "No, not yet." He asked the other people at the front desk and they also hadn't seen them. He put my bags on the trolley and, just as we were heading up to my room, my friend and his wife showed up with their stretch limousine. The hotel worker looked at me like I could tell the future. I told him I was just at their wedding and I knew they were staying here.

Now, I asked myself, what do I do? Do I say "hi" to my friend and let his wife know that I know the "secret location" or get in the elevator before they have a chance to see me? But just then my friend saw me. He had such a big smile on his face so I ran over and feigned surprise. I gave him a hug, wished his wife a "mazal tov" and told the dismayed guy with the baggage to get us out of there as fast as possible. The whole way to my room he kept saying, "I can't believe it. How did you know?" even though I had told him already.

The next morning I looked on my iPad where the closest shul (synagogue) was. It turned out it was a five-minute walk from the hotel and *davening* was starting in fifteen minutes. I asked the front desk how to get there as I headed out with my *tallis* and *tefillin* bag.

On the way I ran into Rabbi Adin Steinsaltz. Rabbi Steinsaltz is one of the greatest Jewish scholars and rabbis of our generation. His international headquarters is right down the street from where I live in Jerusalem. I see the rabbi occasionally on the street and always say "shalom aleichem" (peace unto you) when I see him. What a surprise it was to run into Rabbi Steinsaltz on the street in Manhattan.

He had his head down. I stood in front of him and said in Hebrew, "Rabbi Steinsaltz. Shalom aleichem. What are you doing here in Manhattan? I'm Barak Hullman. I live in Nachlaot." He's a short man. He looked up at me squinting and said, "Good for you," then kept walking.

After arriving at the shul, I opened my bag to put on my *tallis* and *tefillin*, only to discover my shofar was gone. I thought back to what could have happened. The bag had been closed since the previous morning when we *davened* at 770. Then I realized I had left it on the bench at 770. I couldn't believe it; I'd had that shofar for thirty-one years. I blew it every year, and now I lost it and I knew that, even if I had the time to go back to 770, there was no way I would find the shofar. There were countless shofars floating around on the benches and tables at 770. Someone would have thought it was one of the communal shofars and put it in the pile.

My shofar was gone and it hit me hard. It was the only

item I still had from my youth. It was an exercise in letting go of something that was never actually mine. I had about six hours in Manhattan until I needed to catch my flight back to Israel.

The first thing on my list was to get a new shofar. I needed it for the next day when I would be *davening* in the airport in London. After shul, I searched online for the "largest Judaica store in Manhattan." I got an address and headed there on foot.

I reached the Judaica store and asked where the shofars were. There were hundreds of them, all with colored dot price stickers. I had just sold a website of mine a few days earlier for $5,000. I decided I would spend up to $500 on a new shofar. Since the most expensive shofar was $350, I had an unlimited shofar budget.

I first tried some random shofars that caught my attention, but then I realized I had to try every single shofar if I wanted to make a purchase and not regret it. There were over two hundred shofars. I asked the woman at the entrance if it was okay to try blowing all of the shofars and she said that she didn't mind. I blew every single one of them. I started categorizing them based on how they sounded until I got down to three. Then I blew the full *seder* (series) of shofar blows over and over until I decided on the one that I wanted. I took it to the cashier; an older looking woman who was clearly Jewish.

The first thing she said to me was, "Where you are from? You're not from around here." I told her I'd lived in Jerusalem for more than twenty years now. "I can tell right away that you're not from around here. Do you want to know how?"

I really didn't know how to answer her. "Of course. I don't even know what you're talking about."

Then she told me, "I've never heard the shofar blown like that." Then she shouts out to her co-worker in the back of the store and he shouts back, "Tell him not to stop blowing the shofar!" There was a non-Jewish woman standing next to the woman at the cash register. She had this look on her face like she'd just experienced something profound. All I did was blow two hundred or so shofars.

The woman gave me a discount on the shofar and then she told me, "Get on a plane back to Israel today and never come back here again. I don't ever want to see you in my store again. You are too special of a soul to be living in a place like New York." Then she thanked me again for blowing all of the shofars. I left happy that I had gotten a discount and a little confused as to what I did to make everyone in the store feel that way.

Within a few hours I was headed to London to connect to my airplane back to Israel. When I arrived it was early in the morning, just in time to start *davening* again. This time I had my new shofar. It's a little different blowing the shofar in London, Heathrow than it is in New York. But I had to blow the shofar. So, when I finished *davening*, I blew it. I thought, they must see all kinds of strange things at Heathrow. I'm sure they've seen someone blowing the shofar before.

At first I tried to blow it softly, but this shofar has a great sound; an even better sound than my old one and it can't be blown softly. So, I realized, I'm a Jew, I'm proud to be a Jew. I'm getting on that plane in a few minutes. Blow the shofar and change the world. I stood in the corner and blew the shofar as loud as I could. Everyone stopped for a second to see what was going on. Was it an alarm? A fire? It was both. I was both.

www.ingramcontent.com/pod-product-compliance
Lightning Source LLC
Chambersburg PA
CBHW032052090426
42744CB00005B/175